PLEASE HELP YOUR-SELF

Living, Loving, Learning and Preparing the Table

PLEASE HELP YOUR-SELF

Living, Loving, Learning and Preparing the Table

Dale Mary Garratt

New Sound Publishing Ltd
P O Box 28741
Remuera
Auckland 1541
New Zealand

ISBN 978-0-473-49095-9

First published in New Zealand in 2019

Text copyright © 2019 Dale Mary Garratt

Photographs and images copyright Melinda.Garratt@icloud.com
and Brooke Valle-Anderson www.ewalina.com

Cover design StephenJamesHart.com

Typeset by ExPress Communications Limited

Contents

Dedications

To David my love of fifty five years and my dearly loved Melinda Mary the ever faithful one.

To the memory of her sister Rachel now gone for nineteen years or only just a moment ago, and her precious daughter Amelia.

I want to dedicate this book as well to five women who have been with me through absolutely everything imaginable. There is no order of preference whatsoever to your names but I want you to know I honour you from my heart and know you will go on to give and serve as you always have to so many more than me.

As I write this dedication my cup runs over because of all you mean to me.

To Olepa Valle, Pearl Harper, Stephanie Overton, Jayne Burt and Julie Eli.

Interestingly five is the number that signifies grace and that is what you have gifted me with more times than I could ever count. Thank you dear hearts.

With my love
Dale Mary

Foreword

Wm Paul Young

Those who wish to be extraordinary
have rarely first learned
to be ordinary.

With age comes the invitation to remember; to look backwards at one's life and trace the Weaver's threads. Sometimes I see God as the old woman whose dwelling sits at the edge of town. She is the Weaver. Especially at night, people come with their threads, mostly darks and greys, and watch as she adds to them the spectrum of the colors which she stores within her simple abode for such purpose as only Wisdom would comprehend.

I remember in the 1970s arriving at a bible school in central Canada, a teenager in search of meaning and desperate to find a place to belong. For many of us, unless we find someone to belong to, we never belong anywhere. It was this or that person, at this or that time who I now know was a Weaver's thread that kept me alive. And most of them were women. While men had a capacity to give me gifts to engage my end, it was women who entered and exited my life who actually 'saw' me.

One was Ruth Rambo, my Adeline (you will understand as you read this book). She was the wife of the President of the College, had been a missionary in Asia and had a penchant for finding lost children, like me. Ruth was sophisticated in a way that I had rarely seen in my world of modern evangelicals. Insightful and brilliant in a Mary Poppins sort of way, above the fray while being deeply compassionate and wise. It was Ruth that slipped me books, and poetry and suggestions for music, and every so often checked in with me just to let me know that she could see me. Anyone who knew her remembers that she had this remarkable capacity to make you sense that you deeply mattered. Like so many, I still keep her beautifully hand-written notes that would suddenly appear, it seemed, at the precise moment when I needed them so desperately.

A poem by Elizabeth Barrett Browning, a copy of C.S. Lewis's Till We Have Faces, a recommendation for Francis Schaeffer's (a rage at the time), He is There and He is Not Silent and Jacques Ellul's Anarchy and Christianity... threads. One day, in the middle of a prairie winter's freeze, I 'ran into' her. She immediately reached into her bag. "I've been wanting to give you this book for a while. I think it is important and I would like you to read it." It wasn't a book by a theologian, or a philosopher, or a prestigious contemporary cutting-edge thinker. It was by Edith Schaeffer (Francis Schaeffer's wife) and titled, The Hidden Art of Homemaking: Creative Ideas for Enriching Everyday Life.

This wasn't an erudite tome of doctrine, but don't be fooled. Deep theology and truth ran through the pages as Edith explored how to incarnate heavy-headed concepts into the everyday ordinary. What a welcome relief! Someone was talking about God with skin on, about music and hospitality and charity. Ruth was right. In fact, she was protecting me from developing such a large head that I was liable to tip over and hurt someone.

My memory of all this came back in vivid color as soon as I

started reading the pages of the remarkable and brilliant book you are holding in your hands. This is about God in real life, in the bones of the ordinary. But even in the telling, Dale is passing along deep truth. She writes, "It is simply impossible for the young to have 'Old Knowledge'." So true, but especially so in a world where the elders are being shuttled off to loneliness, and the voices of the youth, as wonderful as much of that is, are dominating the virtual world. This is a tragic and certain loss. Like Edith Schaeffer in her time, Dale is doing the same, authentic truth-telling entwined by the words of poets and thought leaders, the scents of blooms and pastry knitted by concepts pulled from worlds as diverse as quantum theory and rock-n-roll lyrics.

The heart of this book, and of Dale's life, is hospitality, the most ancient expression of love, engagement and belonging. Our family refers to Dale, David and Mindy Garratt as our 'New Zealand trinity' (small t), where kindness and care abound, delivered in hugs, music, fantastic meals and conversations that leave you laughing like a well-loved child. In their home and presence, we are seen, loved without question and fall safely into the embrace of their hospitality. It is beyond a gift, ministry or talent; it is incarnational.

I am married to a woman, Kim, who is very much like Dale. They are cut from similar cloth. Those who know them consider them women of earthy and essential wisdom. To them, it is all simple common sense. It is the ordinary. We need these voices to draw us back into an awareness of the Relentless Affection within which we were created, and learn again to live life in extra-ordinary ways.

Prologue

The story I am about to tell you is probably not so far from your own, just a different journey. Hopefully you will get familiar with my tangential way of writing; it's both my story and a self help book… Hence the title.

My hope and prayer is that this life I've lived and what I've learned will put courage, and maybe some understanding, into the deepest place of your heart where your own dreams reside. If I can be even the smallest part of you becoming a more fulfilled person then I am satisfied.

It's a little scary to write from the heart; I am a private person who has lived a public life, but if I don't honestly explain to you how I got from where I was back there in my life – just married and clueless about how I chose to become a contributor to the needs of others – then I would find myself compromising my authenticity. I want to give you the 'why' and 'how' of what happened that will show you what has provided me with a destiny I would have never thought possible.

My skills and knowledge were virtually non-existent, especially when it came to homemaking. So if that's where you find yourself, I want you to know that if I can, you can. I understand there has emerged a global awareness that has altered our mindset about the 'table' and the ways of doing hospitality. Ingredients are more exotic and decor is more eclectic because the world market is available to us now. How interesting to realise that to eat a curry from the hand is if anything a more honest way than with silver service and fine china.

Over these last thirty or more years, our family travelled constantly. Because of that we found out that our own familiar way of doing things could never be the only correct way, depending on where we were. It's been our joy and education to open ourselves to the world and its people. We have become rich in understanding and then a lot wiser when we have chosen to see the unfamiliar without any kind of prejudice. I grieve to think of the ways the more dominant first world cultures have, albeit unknowingly, dispensed with so many of the protocols that nations hold dear, right down, of course, to what and how to eat.

It will always be important for me to have the privilege of sharing what I have with people; for me it's my fulfillment. I believe what Mother Teresa said is very true. She understood humanity so well. I quote:

> "We think sometimes that poverty is being naked and homeless. The poverty of being unwanted, unloved and uncared for is the greatest poverty. We must start in our own homes to remedy this kind of poverty."
>
> Mother Teresa of Calcutta

The essence of all I have to give you comes from my belief system. I have always believed in God yet my understanding has grown more complete as I have come to experience the functions of God in three persons – the Triune God – and in that knowledge I have hugely benefitted.

Since I was a child I have asked God to help me and he has. I have been in awe of his creation; the wonder of it has always been replenished for me over and over by thanksgiving. I am more and more aware of the marvel of how God's grace is always enough, always sufficient, even in my most horrendous moments. I've learnt that if I pause for a bit, and sometimes it takes longer, his grace gives me the courage to carry on; the time to change.

I know too that the hard times will temper me like chocolate when it is heated to the maximum and then cooled. The process increases the shine in both that chocolate and me. I am grateful that in those times when the heat is on I lose some of the burden of self sufficiency, and even the pretension that has inflicted pain on both me and on others.

I know that to help is more healing than to look for help. I know too how we can so easily fail to recognise life's patterns, the gravity of the seasons we find ourselves in, and instead spend our energies giving resistance to that passage. How we fail sometimes to embrace that there is a blessing in the fact that to everything there is a time and a season, and that God makes everything beautiful in its own time.

I've watched swallows assemble and form that ceremonial arrowhead, because they know as summer ends they must leave the eastern shores of our islands in the Antipodes to make their journey across the Pacific Ocean. I've driven down the main street of San Juan Capistrano in California and seen the banner high above the road that welcomes the swallows back home. I've stood in the old mission yard under the bowering bougainvillea vines, luscious in all shades of pink and white and purple. I have watched those scout swallows seek out the places under the eaves where before long they will be joined by their families to nest and rest in the northern spring and be part of this miraculous circle of life they have never resisted.

How can I know which season you are in beloved? All our stories are made up of highs and lows, getting it right, getting it wrong. What I do know is that you and I, by definition of being human, are wired for love and we learn fear. An emotion that can too often cheat us of our God given potential.

I've tried to keep up with technology. There is little bliss in being ignorant. Neuroscience now assures me that I am not a victim of my biology, my DNA or my circumstances. The ardent researcher and neuroscientist Dr Caroline Leaf gifted me the knowledge of neurogenesis, the process where new brain cells are formed each night so that every morning I can imprint on them a positive and optimistic bias. A renewed mind.

The bible says, "The mercies of God are new every morning". Science finally got how it works.

I give to you my 'life' with my love,

Dale Mary

Chapter

1

"The Pleasure of Your Company"

Hospitality

Hospitality – that age old and noble tradition – will for me always be a matter of the heart. To even offer a cup of tea can be a purposeful moment; time enough to listen and make an investment into the soul of another. Something we could have so easily missed had we not captured the moment and given respect to the simplest of rituals.

At school I took a subject called home science. I wish they had taught us that the science in this case could be in fact the connection between people and that a home was a good place for it to happen. I never did learn, after all those lessons, how to make a spectacular cheese soufflé anyway.

Hospitality, if you look at the word, is in fact a hospital, not as we know it to be, but its original meaning is a place of safe refuge even if it's to see people laugh or cry and feel free to be who they really are because they feel at home with you and trust you. Just the simplicity of that can become someone's healing. If we are available enough to be present in a way that brings a certain freedom to a person so they know they are in a loving, safe environment, that's admirable in itself. You don't have to straighten the cushions and light the candles to do that.

I've found from experience that it's being present and available to listen not just hear, so if you can do something to help remedy a situation or network people with others then that in itself makes any effort worthwhile. That lofty prophet Isaiah said of Jesus, long before he came to earth, that he would, "Bind the broken hearted and set the captives free". Such inestimable privileges are ours as we learn how to prepare to receive a heart that might be broken, or a fractured and lonely human, when so many get lost in the shuffle because there is nowhere for them to go.

You may be thinking, well Isaiah prophesied that about Jesus who had the power to do anything. But to me it makes sense of what Jesus said just before his ascension, "I will not leave you alone. You will understand that I am in the Father, you are in me and I am in you". My favourite bible verse. It's worth meditating on those epic words to wring out every last drop because if we have the third person of the Trinity living in us we are enabled to become part of a better life for another.

Mother Teresa was so right when she said there need to be homes prepared, places to go, where restoration can take place. A hospital indeed, but just a different kind where there is food, care, comfort, empathy, and the kind of love that believes the best, that doesn't give up, is patient and above all kind.

The wonderful thing is if we find ourselves out of our depth as we sometimes do, there are always trained professionals who have the skills to put a life back together over a period of time. I believe in therapists and counsellors. Both my brother and daughter are trained in specific areas of need that will always be of great importance to the human condition. In our home we do our best to provide an environment that may just begin with a conversation but may offer a completion as well.

Here then, as I see it, is the 'how' of hospitality, and it is the same for everyone because whatever the question, when it comes to hosting the answer is always the same. Hospitality is about 'them' and not 'us'. At its very best it is a completed cycle that begins and ends with a desire to serve another. And if we really accomplish that, then as hosts we are sure to benefit as well. I've found that is so often the case. When we know this our agenda for hosting is plain and simple. Service, the kind that comes from the heart rather than a sense of duty, is first begun and then sustained through a rule. Not just any rule, it's the one known as the Golden Rule: "Always treat others the way you would like to be treated". It takes us as far 'true north' as we can get.

There's a verse in the bible that really makes hospitality look like a non-negotiable for those of the Christian faith. It's in a letter from the Apostle Peter. Here's what it says: "Practise hospitality to one another, be hospitable, a lover of strangers with true affection for unknown guests, foreigners, the poor, and in fact all others who come your way. And in each instance do it ungrudgingly and graciously, without complaint."

Apparently humanity's most sought after desire is to possess self esteem. This is what I know for sure: I have encountered self worth by putting self second. It is an incredible take out from what can often be a random act and all it requires from us is a heart that cares.

How we harness hospitality and make it ours will always depend on the variables of our culture, our lifestyle and our rite of passage. There is no wrong or right way when it comes to cultural differences. It might be barefoot or stilettos, hands or knives and forks, chop sticks and sitting on the floor. Yes, it all depends... There isn't an answer to how or why people do things differently, so then there is never the question of 'why do they' or 'why don't they'. Because culture does what culture does. Culture is precious to people and never a thing to be judged. The gentle Hawaiians always insist their elders, Kapuna, go first in the food line. In some other cultures I find myself standing back as 'starving' children and teenagers bolt to the front.

Hospitality has filled the landscape of my life from childhood, yet it seems impossible to think I could have been a close observer of the art. When it came right down to it I didn't know for the life of me how it was accomplished or what components were involved so everything would slide together seamlessly in a way that made people feel comfortable and cared for in someone else's home. In this case it was going to be mine. I didn't give credence to the fact that I had never really contemplated whatever it was that needed to come together. It seemed to just happen when people arrived, or so I thought. I had the heart to care – that was never the issue – but how to approach the whole humble beautiful thing of hosting?

I had never given a thought to the fact that hospitality was actually a global tradition woven deep into the ways of every people group on earth. The basics have never changed, nor should they. It is really as old as time; this thing of opening your door to others. There are desert people cooking over a fire and living in a tent, and they welcome wayfarers. In jungles around the earth you could find tribal people who live in huts solving the problems of their world. Maybe that world is a small village but as they talk and eat together solutions happen. For us down under it could be a barbecue in the back yard or simply another place at the table; a more casual approach at times.

I have a penchant for the idea of communion. That way of discovering affinity and trust with someone over a plate of food that seems to capture a certain spontaneity and, if we make room for it, a bequest no other human behaviour does in the same way. To talk, listen, laugh and cry, to share and heal; it's the unwritten agenda of hospitality. I was determined to capture this gratifying art and do it in a way that was uniquely and authentically mine. Ours actually, because David grew up in a home where hospitality was just the normal way of life.

It never should be hard to define hospitality. It's been described as "the virtue of a great soul who would care for the whole universe through the tying together of humanity". I love that thought and the ties that eventuate as people meet and eat. Now half a century on, having made literally mountains of meals for guests, so many feasts and celebrations of all kinds the size of Texas, then washing dishes and doing clean ups for Africa and laundry to the moon and back, I have to say, yes! I feel blessed and gratified that I am at least somehow among the souls that care for what has sometimes felt like the whole universe.

I can't possibly chronicle for you the actual outcome of the ways hospitality has enhanced my life. I have come to know it as one of the most pivotal and rewarding practices imaginable. Any effort it has ever required of me – and there's always some – has been repaid in more ways than I could have ever dreamed of. In actual fact for more than fifty years one of my greatest joys in life has been simply to offer hospitality. I'm going to talk about the art of it but I asked our daughter Melinda to describe her own experience of how she has felt growing up in this way of life.

"Growing up in a wonderful loving home is something I believe I haven't taken for granted. My parents have modelled to me an absolute generosity in everything they do. Whether it's food, finances, their mentoring and teaching, it all goes out from them with an open hand.

"Our family home from my earliest memories was always and still is open to friends, family, and weary travellers. Many times over the years we have hosted overseas guests we haven't known beforehand, but such is the reputation of my mother's cooking. The way she lovingly invites people into her life and home means we have formed some of our dearest most treasured relationships.

"There is a wonderful scripture about always having an open home and offering hospitality because in doing so you may be entertaining angels unawares. I believe we have done that. If not angels, most certainly people who have deeply touched my life as we have sat around our kitchen table just chatting, eating and sharing our stories.

"My mother likes to refer to the 'loaves and fishes' story in the New Testament, and the fact that Jesus so generously catered for the crowds, twelve baskets of food were left over. Her heritage is Maori, Italian and Croatian, all cultures that have such generous quantities of food and love they can always find enough for everyone who enters their homes. There were times we were gone for many months, but growing up in this kind of house as young children and teenagers, our home was always the hub of our circle of friends; never just our family for meals. Hundreds of people have come into our home and I always say if they have gone away hungry it was their own fault!

"One of my mother's delights is to make enough food for guests to take doggie bags home to enjoy the next day. It would never cross her mind to have six people coming for dinner and actually cater for the six only! I can't imagine her counting out pieces of chicken or making only the amount of food needed for that one meal. It would go right against her personality, upbringing and generous loving spirit. One of the sayings she has is, 'As it turns out Melinda, there is always enough to go around'. God's economy has generosity of spirit at its core.

"My sister and I never hesitated in dragging half or more of our church youth group or school friends back home, knowing the fridge was available to everyone and our mother was more than happy to have them all there. Can you imagine how wonderful an environment that was for us kids to grow up in? Such an example of sharing what you have, loving in the most practical of ways, displaying generosity that is like a door always open to God's benevolence and loving kindness.

"I have learnt to give and be open handed with everything I have been given; my clothes, my home, my friendship. It is something I know for sure: the more you give, the more you receive. Saying 'yes' to sharing and giving means receiving so much more in return. I have a little Victorian moneybox with a saying, 'I gather to give and in giving I gather'. There is a scripture that says, 'The one who refreshes another will themselves be refreshed'."

I'm gratified Melinda has adopted this way of living and has reaped the benefits of it. I have no way of knowing where in life you find yourself right now. It would be a shame if you are thinking, 'I don't have a home', and of course that is true for many. Then there are issues of finance, time and where life has you at any given moment. I understand these are very real and genuine situations.

Over the years I've become familiar with the obstacles, yet in saying that I think sometimes what's so easily overlooked is the fact that hospitality is a 'people thing' which means we can share anything we have to offer, anywhere, anytime, any place. If we do the inviting and at least some of the providing then we are still hosting, whether it is in a park, maybe a beach, or at a cafe or restaurant. It is who we invite and why we invite them that matters. Or it could be who just turns up and why. The fact is a home, nice decor, the latest recipes, are all a means to an end, but to give people the gift of our time, whatever the location, is what counts. Even if it seems at times inconvenient and it can be. I know that. Sometimes we have to say, 'let's reschedule'. I've had to learn that too.

It's interesting that hospitable people never find themselves bored or lonely. I've noticed networking and food like each other too. If we can just take a step to offer simple food even from the deli, or maybe a cup of coffee, call in a pizza and throw together a salad, or whatever we feel capable of and have time for, it can go well. Like any choice, it will have consequences and a tangible reward that goes far beyond any sacrifice we could ever make in the doing of it. If it's a food thing, I find people are always willing to bring a dish of something. It relieves the load because sometimes it can be simply too hard to even contemplate the idea of including food. The shopping, the menu, the cooking, the cleanup.

Believe me I understand, I never came to it easily. That letter the Apostle Peter wrote warns about offering hospitality "grudgingly", another translation says, "without grumbling". I have to say earlier on there were times I dearly wished he hadn't said that, for grumbling seemed to help somehow. It takes practice, but I've always gone for at least some simple offering of food because I've come to know the benefits of the difference that can make. We all have a persuasion of what is unique and comfortable for us. It's an estimable goal though, to have people leaving feeling appreciated, nurtured, heard, satisfied, and above all loved. That's why to give credence to this practice and begin with the end in mind will mean our own points of distinction will flourish and people will just come back.

I've come to understand that when I give the best to my guests it will always have to do with preparation. It's inextricably linked to how well things go. Because it's about the gifting of our time, our resources, our energy and of course our emotional bank, I usually prepare well in advance. That way it's easier to reach my cruising altitude. In the end it seems all most people want is to be there with you. So for me this equates to a huge 'how' that has to do with personal disciplines, behaviours – whatever you choose to call them.

I've found it's always going to be about preparation and a workable list, usually starting with what's to eat. With a bit of imagination you can often find all you need right there in the freezer and pantry. If it's planned hospitality that includes food, for me there's always the list. The list comes from what I'm going to serve so I can locate it or go and buy it. If you leave everything to the day your prefrontal cortex, that part of the brain that helps with focusing, can be hijacked. It means anxiety could kick into gear and our valuable brain capacity can be diverted, so in that moment when we need it the information escapes us. If I'm doing anything that will need time and attention, I sidestep the possible panic by thinking and preparing well ahead.

What I came to find out was that the more I offered hospitality the more I knew the truth of the words of Jesus Christ, "It is more blessed to give than receive". It hasn't always been easy because life isn't always easy. Over the years the sharing of my table, my home, or even a picnic rug, for me has required listening at times when I wished I could be listened to, caring when I had a longing to be cared for, making up a bed for someone when I just wanted to crash in a heap on my own bed. We have those times when perhaps our health is compromised or we might be in grief or pain. Life is seasonal so we need to realise where we are and what we are capable of.

I have learned with practice that first I listen to my heart and I am grateful for its reminder for me to treat others as I would want to be treated. What would they like? This way I can go the second mile and maybe make it a little more special. Then I pray what might seem to be an insignificant little prayer but it never fails. I just ask something like, "Please God take care of the rest for me", and it releases that extra bit of wonder that brings it all together.

Once I've done those two simple things that have served me faithfully, then I just do my best. I never go for perfection; the very idea of it sets me up for failure. I just reach for whatever resources my body and soul have to give. Here's a thing about the soul, it will never let you down. Its poetry is one of love and beauty. It speaks to me of many things like candles and flowers so I always find myself looking for the lovely things I can do to enhance the situation. I keep an arsenal of little props and swap them around.

Wisdom has taught me more about the resources of my body, even though it has taken me many years to heed it. I know that one of the most important things I must do is to reserve some of my energy so that I can give my self, along with what else I have to give. This means my meals are simple. I have staples I stick to that I can do quickly.

There were countless times during my learning curves where I felt intimidated and very inadequate to host the people that seemed to just keep on coming. Because of our way of life there have been many musicians, singers, teachers of international fame and even celebrities. Yet I have discovered that people from every walk of life need to be valued because so often it is not only food they are hungry for. One of the best and often unexpected by-products of hospitality is the way it can establish new relationships and take them to another level, while being a means of deepening existing ones.

I've found there's a true fulfillment in the giving of one's time, possessions and of course oneself that has its own profound reward. To invite people to your table with an abundant generosity of spirit, even if there isn't an abundance of food, can be equally rewarding. If your heart is well stocked with abundant encouragement, it can make up for paucity in the pantry, for to put courage into people is to truly feed them. Everyone is satisfied.

I can say without the slightest hesitation that our life's work of teaching the ways of worship to so many groups around the world has been fulfilled through our home being available to host so many people, a lot of whom were strangers to us. Indeed they made a way for us to fulfil our calling to the nations. There are families all over the earth who have become our family and all because of something as simple as these questions: 'Would you like to come and eat with us?' 'Do you need a bed for the night?'

Hospitality is one of the simple singular practices that has changed our lives forever. I have found there are two kinds of hospitality really. One is spontaneous. The other is planned. However I know the disciplines of my basic routines will always give the maximum pleasure and refreshing to my guests. This is something I want to share with you. Routine for me means freedom.

When it comes to the spontaneous, wherever possible it's good to have contingency foods in the pantry. I've learnt the art of being able to throw food together in minutes because whether we slave for hours or twenty minutes, it's our attitude that is always going to be the primary ingredient. Food prepared and presented for the love of it, the love of those who eat it, takes it from an ordinary meal that you want to just get out of the way, to an experience that has the possibility of becoming an indulgence. Basically we receive back the love we put in and often so much more.

I remember in the old city of Jerusalem we bought nothing without a small smiling boy swiftly bringing us sweet hot tea served in ornate glasses at the command of his employer. While we were haggling with a shop owner called Haeill, he looked at Rachel and said to us, "I give you a camel – two camels – for your daughter?" We settled for the tea, and our venerable pianist Bruce Bremner purchased what Haeill assured him was a real camel leather bag.

Being eye to eye, just sharing together, hearing together, maybe resolving together, is surely why we buy the kitchen equipment, the furniture we sit on, the food we eat. It is so much more than just calories and cleanup. Our family always gives thanks to start with. If it was the only meal we'd had for a week, wouldn't we be thankful? Someone preserved the seeds, grew the plants, harvested the crop, and bought and sold, so we could enjoy the bounty. Isn't that enough to say 'thank you' for? The colours, the flavours, the textures, the tastes, the techniques, yes we delight to say thank you to God our provider.

Rituals are very precious vehicles to give us awareness that nothing happens by chance. A shout-out to the Creator will bring more respect for the privilege of provision. As well, in the end it is surely a waste of time to get all the stuff and collect all the recipes if we don't know it's for the love of people.

I understand there has been a shift around of so many things that were once a given in the ways of hospitality. Some of that is probably just as well. I can see why what were once standard expectations are gradually becoming exceptions. In our culture, fewer people include a separate dining room in their house plans because the reality is everyone wants to be near the kitchen, part of the action.

Formality seems to matter less and probably in a lot of cases where the whole family works either outside the home or in a home office, it's too hard and not necessary to do all of the formal stuff. Because I can, I still love to lay the table, almost without exception, even if it's just us. I try to include something beautiful because it's sad to think people get the most flowers at their funeral.

Here's a little piece written by Nikki Denholm who has experienced hospitality in many nations. She is a human rights activist working on causes that involve the deep issues surrounding women and children in particular. In this little story she describes so well how she felt about being around us back in Omahu Road, our family home for twenty five years.

"I first visited the Garratt's home as a young five year old girl, and my foremost impressions still remain with me some forty years on. Arriving at the Garratt's somehow imported you to a wonderful warm and welcoming world that was a celebration to all your senses. Beautiful and delicious food abounding, the sound of worship, the smell of coconut and exotic spices, attention to detail in every room, treasures on the shelves from the family's travels and the ubiquitous flowers everywhere.

"On the guest bed there was always a huge welcoming basket filled to the brim with goodies – soaps and lotions even a spare tooth brush, popcorn, fruit, tropical juices, candy floss, tissues, soaps and supplies that would keep someone going for weeks after they returned home.

"The house was always a whirlwind of people: kids playing, teenagers jumping in and out of the pool, adults laughing, and friends praying and sharing food together. Everyone felt welcome, loved and an important part of this home, that at that minute felt like the hub of the universe.

"The house always seemed very international. Rachel and I would sneak into the guest room where a fabulous speaker or singer from abroad would invariably be staying, armed with books, instruments, a strange accent and, if we were lucky, some goodies that hadn't yet made their way onto New Zealand shores.

"However the biggest remaining impression wasn't the baskets, the food or the wonderful aesthetics – it was how you felt being there. There was a sense of belonging you always knew in the Garratt's home. You were always welcome, and felt special and loved. There was an intangible peace and joy there – warmth and abundance. You never left their house empty handed, hungry or without feeling a little more satisfied in every sense."

In later years Nikki has relentlessly come and gone from many nations and particularly African nations. She has told me of how the village people sometimes have saved a month or more of their supplies, maybe from a garden of whatever they could find, just to host her and her team for a week or so. Hospitality it seems is part of the world's DNA, even in the most fractured places where there is so little to give. I salute Nikki's passion and persistence. She is a rare and resolute woman.

For many years when we hosted people staying for a night or more we never had a guest room, so either David and I or the girls would vacate our rooms. Of course this meant things like making space in the closets with spare coat hangers, clearing out a couple of drawers, depending on how long the people were staying. We are fortunate to have a guest room now and so things are easier these days without all that moving out moving in routine.

In the Owner's Manual on Home, I've described how we prepare a room for our guests along with suggestions that might be helpful for you. Add or take away whatever your lifestyle and budget allows. If you are offering hospitality you are already on the right track so you can really do no wrong, honestly. Follow your instinct; think about what you would like if you were the guest and just go for it and enjoy the process.

When I'm expecting someone I don't know, I'm careful now to ask about different food tolerances so I'm not giving a guest something harmful to their health issues. More and more people seem to want gluten free bread, pasta, sauces and things. Others have taken the big leap and given up sugar. You won't know if you don't ask beforehand so it's always a considerate idea. Some people will bring the foods they eat anyway because they feel safer. I've just gotten into the habit of asking these things beforehand whenever possible and I find people are grateful.

On the other hand if I'm the overnight guest, I find it's easy enough to take along a thank you card because I consider it my privilege to be looked after. I've found it's always considerate to inform people of our daily schedule so they know if and when to prepare meals. I was taught never to come empty handed so it's not on my radar to arrive without something to give, maybe some flowers or a little gift, even if we're just going for dinner. If we are staying for a night or more we always strip the bed and bless the home as we are doing it. We have learned to take particular note of culture because in the Pacific Islands it's no shoes inside (so bring socks if you are a cold footed one).

In our home David has always taken a serious role in praying about who is coming and being conscious of listening to God for something that will be a takeaway for our guests. Maybe just a word of encouragement – everyone needs courage. So here is my story to help you understand the why and how I came to learn about hospitality.

Chapter
2

I let go of her hand and rushed outside,
like the little girl I once was…"

The Beginning

As I made my way up the familiar old garden path, it's cracked pavers now yielding to the deep green moss that had made itself comfortable in the crevices, it was with the anticipation, in fact the certainty, that love and comfort awaited me.

It was one of those astonishingly delicate spring days. Sparkling sapphire sky above, a fresh emerald carpet beneath, and at last those familiar colours you always knew would come back one September morn. Springtime in the Antipodes. Everything seemed to have woken up at once. Blossoms, birds and a repentant breeze that had turned from biting to caressing.

On either side of me as I hurried on, the annual show was under way. Rows of creamy freesias had sprung up and, as they always did, they captivated my senses with their delicious white chocolate scent. All I wanted to do was gather them up and rush them to my face to savour every ounce of their outrageous perfume.

You see I was born on the first day of spring, and as a child there seemed to me to be a certain injustice in having to wait another eternal twelve months for my birthday. Of course now they come with such relentless speed that I'm sure someone is paying Father Time under the table!

Back then I was always anticipating something else as well as becoming another year older. Yet spring is a harbinger that has never really left me after all these years. To see an army of daffodils emerge from their 'big sleep in', you have to wonder how they do the transformation from drab brown bulbs to crowds and hosts of gold, (thank you William Wordsworth):

"And then my heart with pleasure fills
And dances with the daffodils."

You could say I'm a sucker for springtime. It doesn't do it justice to say it in English. J'aime les fleurs, j'aime le printemps. Oh yes I do, I love flowers, I love spring.

I may as well confess right here that by the time I was six years old I had already made a career out of 'stealing' flowers, mostly on the way home from school. Worse still they usually came roots, dirt and all, as I presented them at home and innocently announced that someone had given them to me. My skinny little fingers couldn't break some of the stems so I just yanked them out and stole away.

And yes, to answer your question, I do have the occasional relapse even now. I don't steal, not since I grew up, I just carefully remove stuff if it happens to be in the way of the general public. Come on... even Jamie Oliver says he gets a lot of his ingredients that way. He calls it foraging. People should be grateful that folks like us have such a good public spirit for keeping the outdoors tidy. The whole theory is up for grabs, what can I say? Don't say you wouldn't.

I was carefully 'pruning' a branch off a magnolia tree at an apartment block we lived in a few years back, when a voice – in a somewhat threatening tone – called out the window at me, "What if everybody did it?" To which I solemnly replied, "Well dear, we all know they won't, but it would be nice for them to enjoy something so pleasurable if they did!"

I might have been grinning to myself as foragers do, when my innocent comment transformed that voice into a good imitation of Mariah Carey as it soared up a couple of octaves and screamed, "I'll tell the Body Corp!" PUHLEESE!!! All I was doing, like a skilled arborist, was removing a branch, well maybe two or three, that may have, at least in my opinion, become a menace to passers by.

Here's the thing. When I help people decorate a wedding or some other function, many of them have very limited budgets so I just have to ever so carefully find ways to compensate. Jamie gets it! I digressed from my story – plants, flora, verdure – they make me do that.

I was walking up that garden path remember? By the way I didn't pick any of those luscious freesias, but I inhaled their perfume while I continued towards my destination. I was deep in thought about Rudolph Cvitanovich, that kind and generous man who had lovingly planted them a few seasons before. This man, my father, was that enigmatic adriatic mix that comes from a heritage where men though tough are tender. He was the only man I ever saw in all my childhood who walked home every payday carrying a bunch of flowers for his sweetheart – my mother – and quite often for me as well.

He planted different flowers for us all. He loved the bold colours of his gladioli and I could see why when I went to Croatia and Italy. In his garden were lines of daffodils of every kind and always perfumed roses. Each time I see that winsome lavender bloom called Blue Moon, I'm drawn to the day he planted me a rose garden right under my bedroom window. If I stop to smell one and I do, I'm enfolded with a feeling of the sweetest nostalgia.

When I finally reached the door at the end of the path, I was wondering why my aunt had told me I needed to get there right away when she knew we were due to record. You see David and I had become part of what you might call a 'renaissance'. A long time ago in the 1960s and for about the next two decades, there was a worldwide spiritual phenomenon. It was something of a revolution really. Church people previously involved in their own denominations literally flocked together with no agenda except to worship God, to pray for each other especially those who were sick, and to be taught truths from the bible as were recorded in the Acts of the Apostles, particularly the events of the first church.

Back in that moment of history, people were experiencing salvation through Jesus Christ. They went on to live totally transformed lives, caring for each other, selling what they owned to give to those who had needs, caring for the poor and praying for the sick among them. This resulted in enormous blessings from God. In Acts chapter 4 it says, "They all received the things they needed and God blessed all of the believers mightily".

The 1960s was another unique period when this radical reality experienced over two thousand years earlier seemed to be happening again. People became passionate for truth about their own spirituality. Not only was the Christian community affected, a whole group of young people who before this time had hardly if ever entered a church, came to be known as The Jesus Movement. This 'rebirth' also attracted scores of talented musicians, songwriters, entertainers and recording artists.

It was an age of wisdom and it was an age of foolishness, it was the dawn of a new darkness while at the same time it was a season of light. Thousands of people known as hippies began seeking reality, truth and a new way of life. Many of these 'flower people' followed their idols, mostly musicians (think Beatles), into all kinds of experimental drugs and eastern based religious experiences. They sought a more meaningful life through gurus, drugs and 'free love' that turned out to be anything but free.

Many became enslaved to experimental substances when all they wanted was peace and freedom. Disillusioned and often desolate, some of these people came to experience the amazing grace of God through their newfound faith in Christ. This gift of grace saved so many lost and lonely young people. All they wanted to do was use their talents to tell everybody their own stories of how grateful they were to be alive and free.

The Jesus Movement became epic on the world stage. You may remember Keith Green and his wife Melody who has become one of our nearest and dearest. Chuck Girard from Love Song, our beautiful Annie Herring from Second Chapter of Acts, and far too many more to mention. Some great songs emerged as talent and truth collided.

Everyone had wanted the same thing it seemed. Freedom, forgiveness and fathering, in fact parenting, a clan, a tribe, an iwi, a place to belong. Nothing has changed really. It's what we always want and we always will, for how fragile we are, how much we need one another, how crucial it is for us to be the true and loyal one another can trust to be there for them.

At this time in history David and I, by now with two young daughters, had entered unwittingly on to that 'world stage'. Part of a great wave of worship was beginning to break over the planet. From what one might term the 'uttermost part of the earth', we were destined to ride that wave to degrees we could never have imagined. You could say we were forewarned, and we were very clearly, and you could also say we were 'called' if you like, to be part of its momentum and we were. I'll take you there later.

It basically meant that the two of us, unable to read or write music and barely play an instrument, became totally caught up in that wave to the point where we wrote, recorded and published hundreds of simple songs people could easily remember and use for their own worship to God. Simple verses from the bible set to music. That's all we did. Our talent was so basic and unsophisticated it seemed somewhat audacious to involve ourselves in the world of music. We just put one foot in front of the other.

So getting back to that visit I was telling you about. We were actually scheduled to record some tracks with the Auckland Philharmonic Orchestra under the baton of the exceptionally talented musician and arranger, Bruce McGrail. Once those were completed we would 'lay down' vocal tracks. We were very focused on our task, which was just as well, because that album had the kind of quaint King James English title, "Prepare Ye the Way". Peter Haythornthwaite, the acclaimed designer, illustrated the cover depicting an earthmover as a metaphor of the change taking place at that moment of history in the church worldwide. In a short space of time it became a double platinum recording, as to our great amazement and encouragement, people all over the world seemed to love it and sing the songs in their church meetings, their homes, their cars, wherever. They were so easy to remember, not much more than a jingle bearing a bible truth.

We had already recorded six albums including two for children, and went on to do about thirty six in total, as well as three music books, each containing over two hundred songs. We published several hundred thousand song books with only the words, which were sold in various countries. People are forever reporting to us that they have found translated copies of these books in churches and meeting places in the remotest parts of the world.

So as you might imagine, that particular day on the path my

mind was in two places at once. I was first a mother. I had already seen our children safely to school and arranged for my parents to watch them and give them dinner that night so we could record as late as necessary, but now I'd been summoned and it was urgent.

At the end of the garden path I opened the door, called out "hello" – the familiar ritual – and let myself in. She always sat in the same chair, her black dress a picture of modesty and elegance, except today the chair was empty... Quickly realising she was in her bedroom I hurried in. She lay very still but her eyes lightened and her hands moved as she beckoned me to her.

She was tired. She was eighty six and had been widowed for over fifty years. She had lived through both World Wars and knew the horror of her two beloved sons going to battle. One had been a prisoner in a camp in Nazi Germany. As I recall, although he did return home, he never really got out of prison. Trapped in PTSD, but no one knew what that was, he never got help so alcohol became his only refuge. May we never ever take for granted those who sacrificed so much for our freedom. Single handedly she had raised her seven children; her young husband had died when he was only thirty eight. Not enough knowhow back then to save him either.

In an instant I could see why I was there. All those feelings I would experience over again in my later life rippled through me: the denial, the panic, the pain of knowing but not knowing and, most of all, not being able to prevent the worst. A wave of premature grief washed over me.

Her beautiful silver hair was no longer twisted into that neat chignon at the nape of her neck, the way it had always been in my living memory, instead it flowed way down past her shoulders. She never left it loose in the day, but her inability to prevent what was her obvious decline now seemed to be covering her former elegant and stoic dignity. To me though, she was and would remain my immutable diva. One thing, one classy touch, still remained. She had managed to spray herself with lavender water perfume, her only real indulgence. Everyone gave her Yardley Lavender Water. It wafted around, sharing its herbaceous musky bouquet. It was so much a part of her.

That day, as I knelt at her bedside, I knew she wasn't replaceable. My heart began to flutter and freeze as she looked down at me and quietly said in the words of an old song she loved, "One more river to cross". Adeline always had faith in God and was ready to meet him. She knew it was time to leave, yet her melting brown eyes, a mirror of my own, told me she wanted to stay. I was so desperately torn. She was my teacher, my mentor, my hero, my encourager, my grandmother.

I let go of her hand and rushed outside like the little girl I once was who stole flowers for her on the way home from school. I picked her a sweet fresh freesia, this time from her own garden, and softly walked back to her bedside. I placed it in those tender and once such strong hands that had served us all for so long. I kissed her and told her I loved her, but she knew that because she had taught me to love.

My aunt, who was waiting out in the back garden, told me she died almost as soon as I left. My mind was all over the place as I drove to the recording studio. Just as I arrived they were ready for me to record a song: an ancient scripture written by the prophet Isaiah foretelling the work of Jesus Christ. He said of the Messiah: "The spirit of the Lord is now upon me, to heal the broken heart and set the captives free."

I was thirty three years old. It was the first time in my life my heart had been truly broken, and it was the first time in my grandmother's life she had been truly set free.

Chapter 3

"They do not love,
that do not show their love…"
William Shakespeare

Adeline

It is important that I tell you about my grandmother Adeline, because if it was not for her enduring influence on my life from a young age, I would clearly not be able to tell you much at all. Even though my life was very conflicted, at the same time I was very privileged. However I was well cared for but never taught or trained, the consequences were that when I became a wife in my own home I was bereft – undone and unable.

If you haven't read the prologue of my book you will need to realise it's a tangential piece. I am weaving in and out of my life story with things I've learned that I hope could be useful to you along the way.

So going back to my childhood, here's something I know, in fact we all know as adults: you never really understand what is defining you when you are a little child. Children are wet cement, so impressionable, believing what they are told and how it should be done. It seems to me that the utter preciousness of the gift of a child can be so easily lost in the process of caring and nurturing. It involves sacrifice, but it is the kind that is unquantifiable. Children are a gift that should come stamped 'Fragile handle with care', yet it seems so often they can become the things that get in the way of their parents' and caregivers' ambition. Sometimes they can be treated as what seems like a nuisance, or even worse ignored, as if their value is of no consequence.

I was blessed that I had enough people around me who truly

cared, including my hard working parents, so I never felt like a spare part or an inconvenience. It never occurred to me that it was usual or unusual to be constantly cared for by my grandmother, who was committed to her own and beyond with the enormous drive and discipline of a five star general with angel wings!

I was too young to know if all mothers, like my own, worked at a paid job. In fact as I think back to that time very few did. It was the years of 'the little wife' at home, apron on, dinner ready at five thirty or six o'clock, laundry all done and ironed while she listened to a favourite radio show. Oh, and the baked goods were all perfectly stored – shortbread, fruitcakes, lamingtons, chocolate caramel slices and all kinds of fancy stuff.

Those years in the 1940s appear to have been happening in another galaxy. Even so it seemed totally normal to be raised and nurtured by my grandmother instead of my mother. Later in my teens I received a little culture and refinement from my effusive and very vivacious Aunt Amelia, they called Milly. (Our Rachel named her daughter in her honour.) It was just the way our family seemed to do life. All helping each other out, all doing what they could to be there for each other. Very indigenous as I have come to understand it now.

So my upbringing for the most part was in the more than capable hands of this noble woman Adeline. In this millennium it might be relatives, a childcare programme, a paid nanny or an au pair. Thing is it will always be about taking a village to raise a child and so it should be. Working parents (it might be one parent or two depending on the circumstances) are often tired and unavailable. It isn't necessarily their choice but quite often there's no other way to provide; it's the way it is.

What I found when I began motherhood myself was that by

being open to a sphere of influence carefully vetted, my own children experienced such a richness in their childhood. I was a working mother (writing, recording). In addition to that we spent a great deal of our time on the road doing music and teaching. The girls had amazing, loving, caring input from nannies we took along with us who were all teachers as well. Many of our band members also went far out of their way to love and care for Melinda and Rachel. I'll be forever grateful to all those who picked up the slack, both family and friends.

They even had the constant love and attention from someone who became a brother to them. One of our beloved 'adopted' sons Jeff who practically lived with us, cared for our family endlessly with a selfless servant heart, understanding that the thirty some albums and songbooks we were working on didn't just come out of nowhere. It was hard pioneering work bringing a new kind of music into churches worldwide. For all he did for us, the way he cared for us, he has my deepest gratitude and respect, and always will.

On the other hand my village as a child was really family. Adeline was the most constant influence on me, probably because she was consistent and utterly dependable, believing in values I wish she'd had the time to teach me. Although in my small world I could never have known the gravity of what she was modelling to me. I don't think she knew either, but her innate integrity, compassion and loyalty to her family and her God, to king and country, meant I was brought up, at least where her influence was concerned, to have a reverence for God and to always be true to myself.

In her case she chose benevolence over bitterness and would never miss a chance to use kindness and food for both those who envied her and for many a wounded soul or neighbour in need. I witnessed that as a constant behaviour of hers. An advocate of the non-negotiables laid out for those of us who claim Christianity as our faith, she would quote the timeless words of the Apostle Paul as he addressed an unruly crew in Corinth, Greece (1 Corinthians chapter 13). I quote – so did she:

(The Love Chapter)
"Love is patient, love is kind,
Love isn't jealous, boastful or proud,
It's not rude or demanding when things
are not done its way, neither is it irritable
And never keeps a record of wrongs done to it,
It never approves of injustice
And it never gives up, it never loses faith,
Is always hopeful
And manages to endure through every circumstance."

That right there is enough to make the world go round. Like her, my aspirations are wrapped up in these, the best of human behaviours, the moral high ground. It stuck with me because I realised she was immutable in her values. One of them was tied to how she viewed commitment.

One day she promised me a sewing lesson. I loved to sew from an early age but I left school late, just talking and hanging around instead of making it home on time. She made me hot cocoa and bread and butter – the standard after school snack – then sat me down and explained to me the meaning of reliability, of keeping my word and being trustworthy.

I've never forgotten two things about that. She never admonished or punished me, which was the first thing. Then she explained to me the value of people being able to trust me to do what I said I would. She laid no guilt on me, she taught me instead. I suppose it's that ethic – 'when you get, give... when you learn, teach'. Kids can be foolish; it's not always that they are misbehaving. They have to do foolish things to learn they are being foolish and there are consequences. To this day I have always done the best I can to embrace this – to be a reliable person, one who can be depended on to keep my word.

Well of course it's true our humanity lets us down, but true north is where my compass is set. There is a natural progression that filters through our instincts as we mature and begin to understand about good decisions, good company to keep and how to nurture our conscience because it's a built in warning system. Be very happy when it hurts you and be very worried if it doesn't. In the Acts of the Apostles chapter 24 it says: "I exercise myself to always have a conscience void of offence toward God and people". It's all in the exercising of course.

I'm deeply aware and empathetic of the fact that childhood can be one of two things. It's either largely positive – parents and caregivers for the most part do their utmost to get it right. Or it can be sadly, and too often works out to be, grievously negative, with all kinds of abuse and violation from which it can take a lifetime – if ever – to heal.

Mindfulness and living in the moment is so healing and helpful I've found. It was Jesus who said, "Don't worry about tomorrow", stay right in the day – the moment. I'm convinced that forgiveness goes a long way to relieve us from our wounded conditions. It is particularly true if we have had a negative childhood that can leave us with shame and despair. So it goes that forgiveness, accompanied if possible by reconciliation, will always take us to the high ground.

The media, history itself and even the bible, graphically depict the human condition. Love alone manages to endure through all these things but only if we allow it to. Love can liberate us but the process can sometimes be made up of long and arduous choices, for when the human heart closes, love is the only means of opening it.

I have found to work it out we do well to heed the words of Jesus and stay in the day: "Therefore do not worry about tomorrow, for tomorrow will worry about itself. Each day has enough concern of its own" (Matthew chapter 6). To experience the truth of this for me is staying in the moment then asking myself, "Am I okay right now?" If the answer is, "Yes", then I try to stay in the moment with the mindfulness of the momentary blessings. It's enough for now because gratitude produces fortitude I've found. The other bonus is that we can't be anxious when we are expressing gratefulness; the two just don't work together.

My own progression into adulthood, like yours, has been made up of enormously intricate threads, woven together by the circumstances of how I grew up, what I have been able to resolve and what has yet to be resolved. So you see we really are the same in the end. For all the amazing ways my grandmother influenced me, there remained a mystery that I need to explain to you and I will... later. As I look back and as I look forward, though she has been gone for decades, in another way she is still totally part of my present and she always will be. The bond is there and so it will remain. Like all those on whose shoulders I stand, they paved a way for me. No one hardly ever makes it alone. We, all of us, are the product of generations of the sacrifice, hardship and courageous pioneering of our forebears, people we never met, who in a sense 'paid' for us.

Then there are those we have met and who are still in our lives – our parents, grandparents, extended family and other people of influence who have rescued us and cared for us. These people, especially those whose blood I have in my veins, I honour. Not because they always did it right but because they did their best. They gave me life and therefore a chance to encounter the Creator, the beginning and ending of all life.

Sometimes I think of a certain philosophical point of view my grandmother had. It seemed to show up at times when one of us was disappointed or had made a mistake of some kind that always seemed to me definitive, like the final curtain. A bit of the Italian drama showing up here – it comes out occasionally.

Sadly formal education was one of those things that set me up for what seemed like failure over and over again. The school system and I were foreign countries that never spoke the same language. She knew this. She had never had an education of the

Te Moari Native School
1882-1913

This sketch speaks to me of the huge discrimination my grandmother and mother and their siblings were subject to as 'natives'. Note the spelling of 'Te Moari' which, I can only presume, could have been how the settlers heard the word.

formal kind, but she made sure she learned all the same. So the painkillers she handed out didn't come from any kind of bottle, she would just tell me: "My love, don't go back over what you can't change, it's done". Now they call it 'the rear vision mirror'. You can't go backwards and forwards at the same time. How true it is, yesterday is gone forever, tomorrow, well who knows, so right now is all that's bankable.

She sang a song – Adeline – it went:

> "Count your blessings
> Name them one by one,
> And it will surprise you
> What the Lord has done."

Her version of what could now be called a 'gratitude journal'.

This much I know for sure, it works every time. Gratitude releases grace and grace is the commodity we always need. To name or write down the blessings in a journal makes them stay alive and animate. Even though she did everything to soothe the pain that came and went in my young life, my old life has taught me that some pain never goes away. It has a way of lingering and turning up unexpectedly. It's too late to talk to her about it now but she'd still tell me to count the blessings of it. There always are some, though sometimes, I confess, I have to muster up the courage and just do it.

Over time I have tried to harness what for me is such an amazing by-product of things we encounter like grief, sorrow, rejection and loss (they come to us all). As I have stumbled around in the nightmare of their effect, I have found that compassion has become more of a reality for me and it's mostly come through what suffering I have had; being broken if you like. I've come to know brokenness as a gift that affords me the ability to be compassionate and understand more about what empathy is.

Isn't empathy actually compassion; that ache to help make things better for another? It might lead us to a cause we choose to get involved with that has been brought about by injustice, because deep down we know the feeling of being betrayed and treated unjustly in our own lives. Someone said, "Empathy is YOUR pain that I feel in MY heart." Ultimately it's how compassion works.

Yes, when we know more we do better but everything with all of us is a work in progress. The journey is as important as the destination so they say. I believe that. It has to be said that these words are those of a person living in a developed nation. With every right, a 'developing nation' person could tell me to 'get lost'. For how could I ever understand what it is like to live somewhere like Syria? Yet pain is pain and gratitude is gratitude and they both have their own way with us to different degrees depending on our circumstances. I know them both pretty well by now. I also know that for me there's grace for everything.

It is true I wasn't brought up in a land where there was war, even though I knew something of its effects on my own family. I have never lived in a land of famine, though at times we had barely enough, but always enough. There is not obvious corruption in my homeland, although land and people's identity have been indiscreetly stolen by imperialism. Indigenous conflicts are still not resolved among some tribes. I have never been physically abused – emotionally and verbally with inconceivable rage to a point I had to wonder if I could survive it. But I have no vague notion of what it could be like, as a little girl, to be sold, trafficked, or to live out the unfathomable horror of being sent as a worthless object to evil human beings for their own gain.

Even when I felt desolate in my own situation as a child, I still always had what were more than the basic necessities as well as the luxuries; sweet and soothing things like hair ribbons, flowers to cherish. And when the war ended I got my first bald and beautiful doll I named Crystal. I've never had a scarcity of blessings to count. Gratitude for all I have has thankfully become a deeply healing way that I find helps me to endure pain.

I know I will go on learning. Even as they try to stuff me in the grave I could be saying, "Oh, and can I ask just one more thing!?". I am not vaguely cavalier about people's suffering – that would be inexcusable – but the model I observed from my grandmother, that thing of compartmentalising her own need and looking for ways to meet the needs of others still remains pivotal within me. This has been my decision as well, for I know in the depths of me that I have been blessed in my life far more than I could ever deserve. So to give back is the only responsible thing for me to do.

Here is my favourite prayer that sums up my lifelong supplication and all my aspirations really.

PRAYER OF SAINT FRANCIS OF ASSISI
"Lord, make me an instrument of your peace.
Where there is hatred let me sow love
Where there is injury, pardon
Where there is doubt, give faith
Where despair, give hope
Where there is darkness, shed light
Where there is sadness, joy.
O my Lord and my Master
Let me not look for help so much as to help

To be understood as to understand
To be loved as to love
For it is in giving that we receive
In pardoning that we are pardoned
And in dying we are born to eternal life."

I don't remember a time throughout my long journey that I didn't believe there was a God in charge of the grander scheme of things. Last night I drove to the top of a hill – I'm writing this piece in Kona, Hawaii (yes... I know) – and the sun had gone half way down into what became a golden sea. It was a ball of impossible orange and yellow glory, and as if not to be outdone, the sky was a manifest pink and purple canvas behind it. In front of me stood a large, mature tree, literally covered with stark white plumerias (frangipani) just resting sublimely in amongst the dusky green leaves. The air, the perfume, I could only describe as breathtaking.

The portal of nature has a way of opening the heart to all kinds of possibilities. The big bang theory? There might have been one, but it was masterminded (for my money anyway) by the Trinity who said, "Let us make" and "Let there be". That evening I stood there watching the sun set, feeling like a small piece of a magnificent puzzle, not knowing how to contain myself except to worship my Creator in absolute awe of it all. It doesn't bother me that I've never heard God's audible voice, though I know of some whom I believe have. Nor have I had a sighting of the Father, Son, or Holy Spirit, but isn't that what faith is?

I have had to dig down deep to have any parity with this Adeline, who was a life coach before anyone coined the phrase. I am not sure if she set out to be, she just was. She left no heirlooms because she had none to leave, yet what I have inherited can't be put in a jewellery box or hung on a wall. Living in her presence was like constantly being challenged, as they say, by a steamroller made of flowers.

William Shakespeare wrote, "They do not love, that do not show their love." For she was the only one who always tried to never let me get away with anything that could hurt me later in life, for her ways were those I have come to know as redemptive behaviour. Quoting the 'Love Chapter' again (maybe Shakespeare knew all along), "Love believes the best". She must have seen something in me that I didn't see. She nurtured it with grace, for grace is unmerited and unearned favour, and it is always amazing.

Religion tries to earn the grace and favour of God, but relationship bows its heart and takes the gift.

Chapter 4

"For it is in giving that we receive"

The Blueprint

Armed with the towering influence of my maternal grandmother, one could easily assume that I came bounding into adulthood ready for anything. If anyone had told me that Adeline's accomplishments came through her own personal efficiency and the way she chose, you could say creatively, to manage herself, her time and her resources, I still would never have understood that things don't just happen. Until I was faced with the reality of trying to do what I had seen her do, I was both helpless and hopeless.

When we arrive at what I've learned about food I will tell you everything I know, but I never gave a thought to how her meals always arrived at the table. Simple, rustic, peasant if you like, health on a plate, yet now I think of these meals I realise they were seriously epicurean, although she would never have heard of the word. Everything was like clockwork because she always had a routine. Her food tasted like heaven because she understood flavour, her fresh herbs and those she dried took everything to another level. She mixed up what she called curry spices too. She was a rock star in foodie parlance.

I would see her in the mornings unrolling lengths of fresh white butcher paper over all her work surfaces, then hefting her large weathered wooden chopping board into place. Her old knives were so worn down from being sharpened, they were thin but lethal. She could bone meat or fillet a fish in a flash. I remember when I started working with meats both the piece of meat and I looked like I'd used a chain saw. She mostly had cheap cuts to cook with, so she taught herself exactly how to find the bones, sinews, whatever. Once removed, these would become the basis for another dish in her various and loved repertoire of meals that both comforted and contented us all. She wasted nothing; not a bone, not a piece of peel, not even a lemon rind. "You can pickle anything", she said and she did.

Sometimes on that chopping block there would be crowds of sliced onions, diced vegetables and always herbs – big fragrant bunches. She grew massive bushes of sage, rosemary and thyme, then mint and parsley. You probably know that a long time ago it was mostly apothecaries who used herbs. We all use them now and in this millennium there is much more understanding about the fact that in many cases they are our best medicine.

Adeline always managed a small vegetable garden as we moved from one rented house to another. She grew seasonal vegetables – sweet corn and strawberries in summer, always spinach and silver beet (chard), often potatoes, peas, green beans and waxy yellow butter beans. I remember her coming into the kitchen one day with a smile of satisfaction, her apron held up at the sides, bulging with fat white apple cucumbers. We ate them with sliced onions and tomatoes as a salad with a splash of malt vinegar, along with her rich pickled pork shoulder – they were the perfect counterpoint. Sadly we didn't know we could eat fennel or that pork and fennel were made for each other – to harmonise to counteract the richness of the meat – yet it was always growing wild everywhere, enough to make an Italian chef weep.

The kitchen where she spent hours always had the distinct aroma of comfort from everything she produced. Not only because of her instinct to know how, to taste, to add, to adjust – a little lemon juice here for brightness, another pinch of her dried rosemary there for depth, it wasn't just that – she could do that on a whim – she was all about flavour. But I think, yes I know, she understood innately about the privilege of what it was to truly care for us. That's what I tasted and I still can, it's etched somewhere inside me.

For me to cook is to bring love on a plate. I also feel it when someone, anyone, offers me what amounts to the best they can do; a gesture for my family or me. I don't think about how epicurean any meal is. I don't care if the flavours aren't right, if they don't go together. What I taste, what I savour, is the effort someone has gone to; the something that remains long after the meal is finished. It makes love the star and food the supporting act. When I am given someone's time and resources, I always find these gifts immensely restorative.

There are those in my life – some women, some men – who deliver into my heart that same thing my grandmother did. It's the knowledge that I am chosen by them to be loved. Some of them are among the best cooks I know, including dearest Jan, my tireless editor. Others are at all stages of experimenting with the idea that it's not just about food and ambience, a candle here, a flower on a platter there, that makes things perhaps more memorable, it's about how much one cares. To cook because you love is to make an unforgettable choice for the receiver, who leaves with more than a satisfied palate. Hospitality is a restorative and healing practice. Hospitality means the hospital is functioning with more than food.

This is why I love what Saint Francis said: "For it is in giving that we receive," there is an irrevocable truth contained in those words. Once we know that we know it, we are somehow freed to live our life with an open hand. It introduces us to well being – being well – within the very core of us. Our body that carries around the authentic 'us' may never be completely functional. It is a challenge I'm familiar with, but the true essence of us can always discover and rediscover the joy there is in giving.

Interestingly enough, I've found happiness is a by-product that comes from the joy of giving. It is a positive psychological emotion that in the end results naturally in our lives and remains even as we clean the last dish. It's the final deposit of joy and the gift of satisfaction. I can tell you that because like so many of you, I know that I know the truth of it. Food for me, as it was for Adeline, will always be an expression of how much I love, how much I care. The why before the how. If there's a why we can endure almost any how. The pursuit of happiness is, I believe, to give oneself away.

Experience is my teacher. Scarcity and being afraid to give can become a form of toxicity – it's true any fear demands a price. It's not always logical to blow the budget or give your last cent. Jesus said in Matthew chapter 6, "Your father who sees what is done in secret, will reward you". I could write a book on my experiences of that theory alone. So Adeline showed me something about that. If I have regrets (and of course I do), one would be that I can't sit down with her and say, "So, what about all those conversations we had without speaking a single word?"

The landscape of my soul as a child was continuously changed by my observations of her. Poor and rich all at once, just living to give herself away. Self pity or being a victim was never her modus operandi. God will always see to it that we have enough because in giving, we receive. I knew Adeline owned kitchen knives, a sewing machine and some clothes she made for herself. I don't think she had any jewellery other than a cameo brooch and her wedding band, and never a bank account until she collected her meagre pension as a senior citizen, but here is what she had.

As I ponder it you could never put a price on it, but a value, yes absolutely. She was satisfied with what she had. To be satisfied is a rare and truly fulfilling experience – to really know that enough is precisely enough. I am persuaded that is what true satisfaction really is.

I don't think it comes naturally to be content with what we have, but in the developed first world it's enough for right now. A scarcity mentality inevitably results in the worry that we may never have enough. We cling fearfully to what we do have, and the 'what ifs' result from that thinking. To practise being mindful of the moment rather than focusing on what's gone before or what lies ahead, both options are a slippery slope. In my experience there is always enough grace for now. "Grace for now, grace for a day."

Adeline's paradigm, that habit of counting her blessings, was her personal discipline of gratitude. However our mind works, it turns out, I repeat, we don't have the capacity for gratitude and anxiety at the same time. Gotta love that. I'm thinking that being thankful could solve a lot of problems because it delivers us into the now, and that's the only reasonable way to experience grate-full-ness. For me, it's practising these things as habits, pondering the positive. It takes time and effort but all habits form with practice, and remember perseverance will take you there.

For Adeline it was only ever about what she had at the moment to give away. With all she had lived through and was living with, there must have been horrendous pain and so many things beyond her control, yet she had come to some place deep within herself where she was satisfied with whatever she had and it was from there she offered herself to others. I have come to the conclusion that a mind thinking about what we don't have means there will never be enough. I have noticed, especially with the giving of hospitality, that some people wait and go on waiting until they get the new table, better equipment for the kitchen, whatever it happens to be, when no one really cares where they sit, or so much about what they eat; they would rather be there being loved and heard.

Sometimes Grandma let me stand on a chair to stir a pot. It is true she never wasted a single thing. She seemed to handle food with a sort of reverence; meat and poultry were scarce back then. We were never too far from the ocean so there was always seafood. When it came to beef, the bones became an aromatic bone broth or soup. How could anyone make something out of nothing? Stirring a pot of bones that cooked for hours and hours never made sense to me, even with an onion and a carrot floating around amongst some herbs.

But I still remember the smell of something heavenly as I came near the house on a cold wet day after school. As she dried my long curls with a scratchy towel sun dried on the clothesline, I almost inhaled that soup, the bone marrow floating around amongst vegetables and maybe some barley. Of course now the nutritionists tell us if we want to make it through the toxic maze of sugar, carcinogenic additives and genetically modified foods, just about our only hope is bone broth! Who knew?! You'd have to say Adeline did – even though she didn't!

She preserved every piece of fruit we didn't eat in the summertime – everyone had fruit trees. My mother helped her when she wasn't working; they would peel peaches and apples for hours. The shelves would be packed with bright Golden Queen peaches, green and yellow plums, apple jelly, strawberry jam, and jam made from luscious dark purple satsuma plums right off the tree.

When I was really small she made her own butter with milk that was almost cream. Her friend had some cows so we would go to his house and get jars of fresh milk with a rich, deep layer of cream on top. She would sit with the bowl on her lap and churn the cream with some salt for what seemed like forever, until suddenly a big lump of butter appeared, golden and silky. It was wrapped in wax paper then rushed to the icebox to keep it fresh.

The icebox consisted of a wooden cabinet with holes at the base and a zinc tray underneath. The large block of ice would drip through the holes to the zinc tray you would empty as the ice melted. This was our fridge and freezer! The great big ice man did a delivery every week in his van full of massive ice blocks that he secured with leather straps and set down in our icebox.

There's no time or need to make butter now unless you're Amish, but I often think Adeline accomplished more in a day than many people do using automation. She always had a daily plan and often made several meals, or at least the start of them, at one time. It works; it's just called 'being prepared'.

Once in a while my uncle won a raffle at the local pub. He would bring home fancy meats; pork for roasting, a leg of lamb and even oysters and crayfish if he played his cards right, and occasionally he did. Why it happened was a puzzle to me as a kid, but Grandma would share the good stuff with friends or relatives who were always around. My uncle didn't care, he ate at the pub, but sometimes I would groan inwardly to see half a pork roast with its crisp crackling on top and the best golden roasted potatoes go right out of the door, carried in the arms of that woman with the abundance mentality.

It was sad though that there were no expectations on me to lift a finger. So no, I never learned how to manage myself, my possessions or – of major importance – how to contribute. My admiration for her was immense but I never got the blueprint. The how. It seemed no one had the time or headspace to think of teaching me about things like food and how to prepare it, or day to day stuff like laundry and chores – to be a good steward of my possessions and other people's as well. None of that was even a vaguely familiar thought to me.

It then goes without saying that I had to drill through the hulking rock of inertia to teach myself constructive behaviours. That's some rock! Sewing I could do. Did you want a dress? No problem. Some eggs? How would you like them? Burnt or more burnt? A place for everything, but nothing in its place? You'd have to send out a search party to find my other shoe once David and I set up house.

So I'm thinking is there anybody out there who would like to learn some stuff and save themselves from some of the hazardous terrain I've hacked my way through? There's the good news and then the not so good news as life rolls along. The lesser for me is that I'm at the end of my seventh decade. But hey, the good news is that I have a lot of accumulated data and I have no intention of withholding any of it. Some of it, I'm pretty sure, could be helpful to someone.

As I have said there is a 'why' we do everything and then a 'how', because from my own experience I know it is possible to achieve an even half way good result by being organised enough to be the one who is available to care. Of course I fully realise some truly do care but they have totally valid reasons why they can't be available, and I empathise with them. I've had enough traumas to understand.

However I've come to know that preparation is a huge part of the success of most of my endeavours. For me it makes the end result so much more achievable no matter what the task. Once I finally put systems and behaviours in place it became much easier to be available to others. I will tell you how I learned all of this. Choice after choice, decision after decision, courage. I had to drag it up by the boot straps! Talk about a sorrowful spoilt mess that was me, no kidding, and if it's you, we can fix it.

Everything is incremental, patience with oneself is a good friend. The thing I did have was a role model and at least I could see how it all worked. The other weird and wonderful upside to my formative years is that for much of my other life I have slowly begun to realise that some things have come naturally to me, things I was never taught. Another reason is that I read because I always want to learn. You will probably already have found that to be true as well, but the art of discovery is something I would love to explore with you. Curiosity is a wonderful path to tread. Once we stop being curious about life, we somehow halt our learning process.

You will also know as I do that certain ways become part of us. It can happen almost entirely by osmosis as it did with Adeline and me. Her influence, though not necessarily deliberate, was my teacher. I have to concede they didn't call me Dale Mary Adeline for nothing. Children, it appears, learn three fundamental things.

1. They do what you do.

2. They do what you do.

3. They do what you do.

If you don't already know this you may come to find out that it's only too true.

I guess I've always looked for role models, even though

sometimes I have found it necessary to reinvent some of their ways of being and doing. Right here though, before I go on, I want to say that the content of what I share is by no means only for women. Men have been amongst my greatest teachers. I have always looked for men I can include in whatever I do, and at the same time I have taught them things like how to cook, to entertain and to generally use their creative skills. Over the years it has made me proud as they have gone on to exceed my talents. It is so gratifying to draw new skills and abilities out of people who always thought they never could. I'll show you what I mean.

Last September I received this letter from our precious 'son' Luke. He is the one who put my lyrics to music on our album "Coming Home". This man is not only multi talented, but a super humble human being who has used his own suffering to heal others as well. Here is what he wrote to me on my birthday:

"Beloved Dale,

I honour you and my family honours you with much, much love. Your life examples to all of us are so many things that make us live and serve well. I see you in the way we offer hospitality and have people in our home, and now I see you when I go to my daughter's home. The integrity you have to be faithful to your convictions, values and beliefs constantly inspires me to live the best that I can and share my life generously. "Last night, with people at our table, we remembered that you taught us to do it with class and a heart to bless. Your legacy is strong and lives in us and I wanted you to know that. We owe you so much and are so grateful for the mentoring, leadership and life that you

tirelessly share with us.
Very much love,
Luke."

The fact that he learned from me and put it into practice made me weep for joy.

I will never forget the simple act of hospitality given to me in my own home by another man whose friendship I treasure. Stephen is mostly known for his exquisite gift of music, but he is in many ways a gentle shepherd who saw me undone, unable to bring food to the table, wrestling with the loss of my daughter the day after her funeral. He was very close to her so it was painful for him too, but he quietly prepared and made his offering. While not even knowing I was hungry, I became so gently sustained and healed by his kindness.

He sent me a birthday greeting last year as well – a Facebook message with a photo of our mutual friend and consummate musician Andrae Crouch playing on Stephen's piano. The photo took me back to when Andrae himself had invited us over and made our family southern fried chicken in his own kitchen in Hollywood. I honour his memory and the music he gave us all.

My good friend Kevin is not only a superb self taught chef, he's what I call a 'second miler' and that's rare! Recently I was at a dinner at his home where he not only cooked the most succulent pink lamb, he served about twenty of us (all women) with such panache. When I went out to the kitchen to help with the clean up it was spotless. Of course he would do no less. I know from experience it's a big ask, and yet his attitude was unflappable, he had loved doing it for us all.

The world is finer for these men and so many more I really want to tell you about. Their music, their hospitality – I haven't got room to name them all – but they have been men who never shrank back at cooking and serving my family and me. You know who you are, my beloved men friends. My editor won't let me name you all or we will have the Encyclopedia Britannica.

However there's an octogenarian, my dear friend Roly. Every year his beloved wife Claire made us a superb Christmas cake, beautifully packaged and covered in love (many of the ways of hospitality I learned from her). After she graduated to heaven, Roly decided to take on the challenge and turned up at our home the next Christmas with a perfect cake he had made all by himself.

As I write it hasn't stopped there. This veteran missionary, a truly perennial sage, has taught himself to make all sorts of wonderful food. How many men do that when they are eighty plus? He has truly seized his senior day. And now he is out and about finding people he can give a gift to. As an evangelist he is giving away the Gospel of John to whomever he finds in the mall or on the beach. To me he is Saint Roly.

Jesus himself, of course, showed what the abundance mentality could really be like when it comes to hospitality. I love that when he fed people there was always so much extra food it had to be gathered up by the basket load. It works for me; people just take it home. His disciple John tells the story of a mindboggling catch of fish they got not long before the actual ascension of Jesus Christ to his father.

The story goes in the Gospel of John chapter 21, that the men were out fishing about three hundred feet from the shore. As they got closer they saw a fire burning on the beach and fish were frying. Jesus was alive again and called out to them, "Bring some of your fish and come here and we will have some breakfast". You have to say it trumps throwing another shrimp on the barbie. Turns out they could hardly haul the net in it was so full. It was hospitality on a Mediterranean beach with the Master Chef.

Another man who is very dear to our hearts is Paul; you will have read his foreword. Of course he is author of "The New York Times" bestseller "The Shack", and other amazing life changing books that are essential reading. What I want you to know about the real him is that not only does he write handwritten thank you notes when he stays with us, he strips the bed, folds the blankets and covers, then brings the sheets to the laundry. He would wash them as well if I didn't stop him.

There is a common denominator here. These few men I have mentioned possess such humility and generosity of spirit, yet what makes them so exceptional to me is their kind hearts and respect for women. Sadly I know too many to mention, as I said, but I have the deepest respect for all of them including my own brother George, heading to ninety and cooking up a storm – always in debilitating pain, always willing, loving and caring.

It is interesting to me that some of the men I know well and many of my women friends have stories just like my own. Their insecurities and difficult beginnings could have held them down also to where they would never reach out to others, but their courage has prevailed and made them into some of the greatest people I know. So many around the globe are my lifelong friends.

On the weekend of Rachel's burial our most loyal Landa, a missionary flying from Florida at a moment's notice at her own expense, literally saved our lives doing food, laundry, everything for us. How our family loves her. Men or women, it doesn't matter, it's how or why they do it.

And you can do it too. I truly hope it doesn't sound trite when I say it, but what I'd love is that you can sense I actually care about the fact you are taking the time to read this. It makes me hope you might reach out for more of your own potential, the best and most authentic you, the one you alone were created to be that no other living soul can replace.

I understand we are all made of the same stuff but yet made in the image of our Creator God, so yes we are enough right now and we will be better if that's our heart's desire.

Rudolph Cvitanovich with son George.

Noel Garratt with son David.

Mindy with some of the Garratt cousins.

Cousins Mindy, Jacqui and Rachel.

Jacqui, George, Cathy, Shelly and Beryl Sweet.

George and Dale, siblings.

Dale aged 6 with mother Florence and father Rudolph (on right).

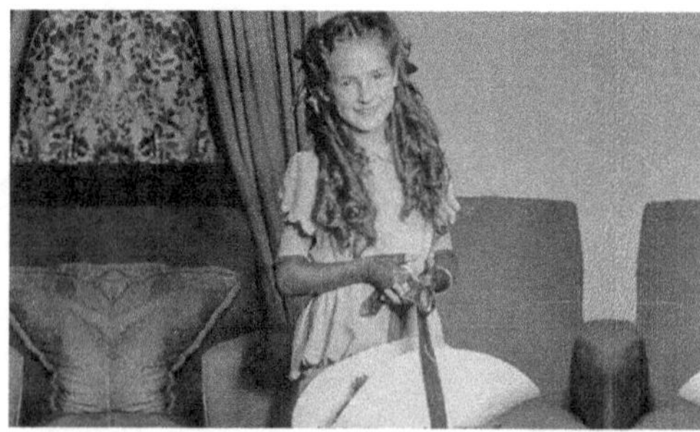

Dale Mary, bridesmaid.

David and Dale's wedding day.

Revisiting 1 Brent Street, Dunedin.

Rachel's wedding, Dale calling the Karanga.

Rachel on the beach.

David and Amelia.

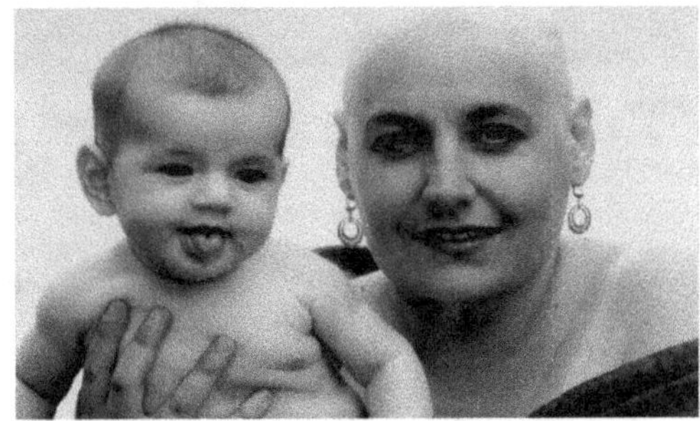

Rachel and Amelia during chemo days.

Ihaka and Amelia, grandkids grown up.

Amelia and Nan hugs.

Chapter
5

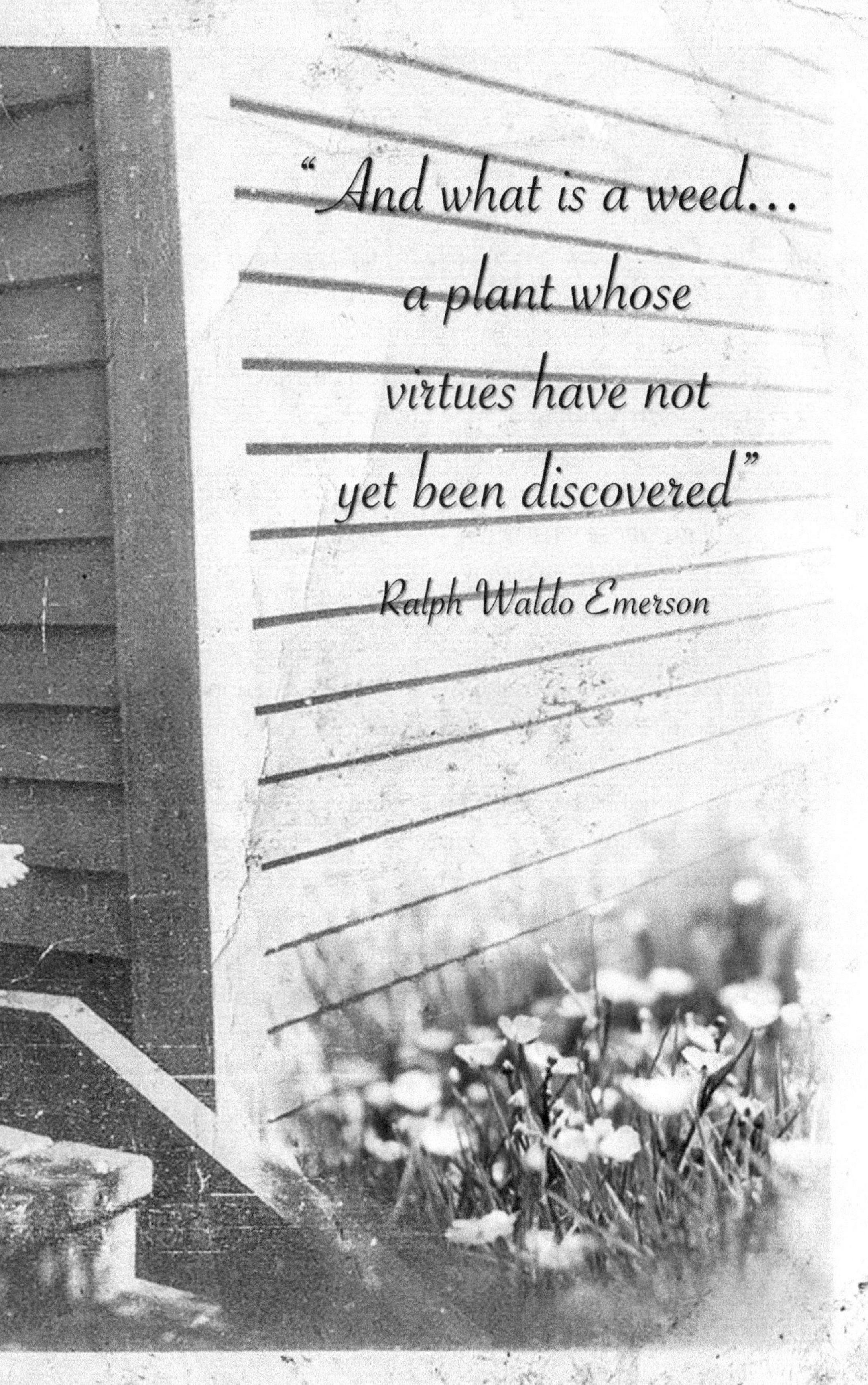

"And what is a weed…
a plant whose
virtues have not
yet been discovered"
Ralph Waldo Emerson

Dale Mary Adeline

Here's an interesting thought; it's simple, has potency and is certainly worth pondering:

> "And what is a weed,
> a plant whose virtues
> have not yet been discovered."
>
> Ralph Waldo Emerson

I agree with whoever said, "It's kind of fascinating that a weed might seem to grow right out of a rock. You can't imagine how it survives how it is nourished, how it thrives. You may even think when you tug it out that it's gone forever... but next year there it is... back again! There's a lot to be said for perseverance and courage; they become our playmaker over and over again."

I love what extraordinary Brené Brown teaches us about how we can rise up and regain our strength with "skinned knees and a bruised heart". She is someone you want to get to know through her books and YouTube. I've learnt that when we try to ignore our struggles and turn away from them they still own us. Our freedom is jeopardised. You can pack your bag and go anywhere and they will go right along with you.

There is so much I have learnt from having my heart broken over the years, especially by those I have trusted to believe I was always trying to do my best. Yet I know for me compassion has pushed through my pain and somehow surfaced. I'd say I've learned the meaning and function of what grace is from disappointment, and gained so much more courage from the times I've failed and had to try again and again.

One of my heroes Maya Angelou said, "You may not control all the events that happen to you but you can decide not to be reduced by them". I wish I'd known that sooner. I suppose we go on discovering things about ourselves endlessly, and it's true other people in our lives can sometimes discover our gifts for us. That has certainly been the way it has worked for me, mostly because I saw myself more like a weed than anything useful. I lived a long time under the assumption that if I wasn't an academic there was no way for me to be useful, to succeed or to be clever in any subject except home science, as it was called back then. The way of being taught in our school system disadvantaged me.

It's not my intention to tell you my whole life's story (yes I know you're grateful!). But for me to have achieved anything much at all, like many of us I have needed those on my journey who have remained with me after realising I am not and will never be anything approaching perfect. To those who left and never gave me another chance, I'm sad I didn't and couldn't do it better. No excuses: your best is all you have at the time. The 'power of one' is the admirable exception, but for most of us there's a need for someone to cheer us on and go the distance with us out of sheer love and loyalty. It's exactly how God treats us. Neuroscientists tell us we are wired for love, and of course we are because we are made in the image of God.

The generosity of spirit of many has helped me survive the times when I have been so crushed and felt so inadequate, as we all have, yet in the end it is always the way more fragrance, nourishment and compassion works its way out of us drop by drop. "We are all just walking each other home" (Ram Dass). So true, and when we give up on someone it's usually our loss because for all of us, grace gives us the time to change.

Enigmatically what looks like a weed can end up being something amazingly beneficial, with healing properties that can be made into a marvelous elixir, a fine and fragrant wild mint or dandelion tea that sustains and heals. I have to say, to my amazement really, I have found that over time I have been able to develop something approaching my grandmother's virtues – I'll call them behaviours. These have gifted me with some staying power of my own to rise at least at some stage after I fall and be there for others.

The altruistic people who have journeyed with me will always have my gratitude and loyalty – David and Melinda, as you could imagine, being my chief encouragers. Just this past Mother's Day 2018, Melinda wrote me a card. She was wearing her rose coloured glasses, but nevertheless we all need this unsolicited and beautiful affirmation to make it through the mountainous terrain of life. I quote:

> "My darling Mama,
> Kind hearted and so thoughtful, you are incredibly generous putting me before your own needs. You continually go out of your way to serve so many, to put others at ease and enrich their lives. I could write a book on how many wonderful life changing and long lasting things you have taught me. Your relationship with the Triune God is alive in you and it shows. You are loved deeply by hundreds and hundreds of people

all over the world. I honour, cherish and love you this Mother's Day."

I know she's my daughter but it helped to affirm in me that I'm not the weed I once thought I was. I dare not begin to name a host of others. My ardent encouragers.

Of course without a doubt the grace of my God will always be my sustenance for without it I cannot function, there is no true me. I said it in some lyrics I wrote in a song talking about God. I described him as, "The very breath I take". My own self given mandate then, is to hand on to you the good, the best I have. It is by no means all the things that will complete you, but at the very least it may be an encouragement to you. If I could give you some ways I know that really work for me, then perhaps some of these things might save you from wandering around the great abyss of unknowing as I did.

I was, like so many of us, doing the heavy lifting, carrying with me so much that was unresolved. By the time I was in my twenties I was very adept at blame shifting. It was easier to recall my circumstances – how I was raised, how I was schooled, how I was marginalised and how my knee became so injured that I would never be able to follow my life's grand dream to become a professional ballerina. It all meant that the ingrate in me – in other words my lack of gratitude for what I did have – was looking for consolation. "One Thousand Gifts" by Ann Voskamp is gratitude on wheels.

What is it with us that we find comfort in feeling sorry for ourselves. Well I know now it's our ego – that thing that makes us keep thinking about ourselves. I have had to train myself not to be that way so I know it can be done, for the most part anyway. I could always find a good reason for why I was the way I was and who I could blame. But however true that is, it 'red cards' you. You leave the game, you no longer take responsibility for your own decisions or, worse still, your own destiny. Someone else has caused all your problems. Yet our excuses will never be our solution to moving on.

Even though I had felt very inadequate for many years, something shifted in me to where I no longer wanted to be the way I was. I wish I could say I was motivated by the recognition that if I was ever going to be vaguely like the person who had been my role model and influenced me so profoundly there was only one way to get there. Courage and perseverance. I had to do what we all have to do: the hard yards. It was the fact that I needed, with God's help, to fix myself.

No one else can really do it for us. They can give us tools and that's efficacious, but the responsibility to change ourselves belongs to us. To quote that eloquent Franciscan priest Father Richard Rohr:

> "Spirituality seems to be more about unlearning than learning and when the slag and dross are removed, that which evokes reverence, the goodness of God, fills all the gaps of the universe, without discrimination or preference."

After all it's the grace and kindness of God that leads us to repentance… to change.

I'll give you a close look at how things changed for me, but basically I reached for the sky and landed back on the ground. Not necessarily where I wanted to be but in a better place than I was before, knowing I could get further along the road to restoration.

An indomitable mentor of mine Stephen Covey, author of "Seven Habits of Highly Effective People", sums it up:

> "Sow a thought, reap an action; sow an action, reap a habit; sow a habit, reap a character; sow a character, reap a destiny."

Read his books if you can, he sure left a legacy that put me on the path to change so many things about myself. I am forever grateful for this laudable man.

Now as I write a big part of my motivation in being here with you, beloved, is because I can never know if you have someone who has stuck with you, waiting until you have regrouped, telling you to 'hold on it's going to be okay, nothing lasts forever'. Right from when I made some life changing decisions, when I felt I had little control over my life, it took someone to notice my dilemma and give me a gentle nudge in the right direction. I had settled into a comfort zone of rather listless lethargy and self pity. I had told myself a miserable version of what I thought my life was like.

For my dreams and ambitions to become a reality, it took a certain feeling of humiliation and even disgust at how and where I had ended up. It would probably make you cringe because I had certainly reaped myself a character that I was not at all proud of. I wasn't trying to be some version of Angelina Jolie with a bit of Oprah thrown in. Actually to begin with I was just wanting to know where everything was in the chaos of my new home so I could try to do something with it. I can hear that look!

I have to say regarding Oprah, the way she's shared her life and knowledge so openly has introduced me to some incredible teachers and writers. She's also modelled for me how from what seems like her impossible beginnings, she has had the courage and willingness to be vulnerable in the most public of settings. Talk about a hero. What benevolence and depth of spirit.

As I listened to the last episode of the Oprah Show some years ago she clearly credited Jesus for what he had enabled her to do. She spoke freely about the grace of God, in fact she virtually preached to the audience about how God had enabled her to become a contributor. You will be inspired to hear her speak on YouTube. It's why it's so important to have role models and examples to follow.

Could anyone with all my advantages be so disadvantaged? Well yes. The way I arrived slowly from just having dreams and ambitions to some semblance of reality is what I want to tell you about. It is of course the 'why' of caring as I have come to know it. The caring for some of us comes naturally, then again for others of us, and especially me, all the dreams and ambitions in the universe never got me from A to B. It came, as all the good stuff does, with a price tag. Doing as well as dreaming.

Who knew there was an A or B to get from one place to the next! Well I sure didn't. Partly because of World War II and because of the fact it was on the heels of the Great Depression, the atmosphere of my childhood was one of uncertainty and fear. Grownups glued to the radio, just waiting. Maybe a dreaded knock on the door, never knowing what the news would be of a loved one lost far away in some horrendous battle. Yet no one talked about it or explained it to me, they did their best to shield me from reality.

As far as I can figure out looking back, I'll tell you another reason why I was so disconnected as a child and how that eventually landed me with a dented and buckled self esteem. I was different from many. Obviously not vaguely close to being as disadvantaged as many others I see every time there's breaking news around the world – the horror, the real horror for those who are unable to escape from how they live. Mine is not a three hanky story – no need to get out the violins – it's just your 'normal' dysfunctional family. Why did they argue and get drunk? As a child I had no understanding of their stories and I never knew how much they were hurting.

I'm going to give you a trip back to school with me. In doing so I want to make it very clear that although those years were traumatic in many ways, I'm profoundly grateful to be among the women of the world who have had the gift of education and unlimited opportunity. It's not something I could ever take for granted. Neither had I ever realised I was made in the image of the God of creation, so my DNA had the essence of creativity ready to be tapped into any endeavour I chose.

In the five years before I started school everyone in the family spoilt me because they wanted to shield me from the relentless suffering a war brings. But kids know when things are out of whack and adults are doing their best to cover up. Conversations were always going on about who had died, been maimed or become a prisoner of war. There were many tears and heartaches, so much loss and grief. War is such a grievous thing that changes so many lives forever. No one seemed to realise though that I suffered just watching them suffer. It was a rollercoaster too big and fast for a child to get off.

So starting school I was apprehensive, disquieted and unsettled on one hand, while being totally optimistic and keen to learn on the other. Yes, the weed with virtues ready for the using. Sadly though, the school system – learning in the way I was taught – was my nemesis. I was and have always been intuitive. The term 'emotional intelligence' wasn't known back then, but I was fearfully aware I never possessed any kind of academic intelligence. Many of us in Polynesia have had the same struggle with being forced to learn in a way foreign to us because we are visual learners. Thankfully it's being taken into consideration in this millennium.

There was another situation I found myself in. Long ago when I was young, just a little brown girl with long brown hair and dark brown eyes, all I knew, all I felt, was that I was different from everyone else at school. So from deep within me a question arose. No matter how perfectly presented they made me (and they did), each time I walked through the big iron gates to my school, I became assailed with the feeling – the uneasiness – of how different I was around those beautiful blue eyed, golden haired Aryan girls and boys. Some had freckles I secretly wished for. (Who knew that much later I would marry a Garratt, a very freckly David Garratt?)

There was a shy Indian boy about the same dark colour as me, and it always seemed that everyone ignored him. Some people (I'm sure I was thinking) were lucky enough to win the biological lottery, but not me, not him. It was too late for that... or too soon: now you can even say, "Guess what? I'm learning Te Reo Maori". Our native language was disrespected when I was young and outlawed when my grandmother and mother went to school.

How could I know the future was going to be more colourful. Indigenous peoples are now celebrated for their cultural differences, at least to a greater degree than I could have ever imagined. Yet there is still a long way to go. So many wrongs to right that even the land, the precious whenua, cries out for justice. So much innocent bloodshed. For me though it was too wrong. Right there began a need in me for my peers' acceptance. If I was the wrong colour, the only way I knew to integrate with the others was to invent ways to get attention.

I laughed out loud when my teacher fell right through her chair and went home with welts on the back of my legs where the senior teacher took his leather strap and punished me severely. Although forbidden, I chewed gum in class just to be smart. It was Juicy Fruit, a new amazing thing we had never seen before the Americans brought it. I was severely punished again for my bravado. Later I learned Her Majesty Queen Elizabeth II tells us a lady never chews gum.

I was ten years old and began thinking that if I cut my long hair maybe I would fit in better. I was left with the regret of a stupid decision and still didn't look like any of the others. After the summer vacation I always came back to school an even darker colour. I was shrinking into the swamp of insecurity. I knew nothing of racism or that it was even a word. What began in me from my early years was a quest that lasted a long time; to know who I really was and why I was different. It was socially unacceptable, even as far along as the forties, to have mixed blood, particularly indigenous blood. A half caste, as I was referred to, was considered a lesser being and it made me feel inferior in every way.

So my formative years and the subject of why I was different came up quite often after school. The question was always the same and the answer never changed either. With my mother at work, it was usually something I tended to ask my grandmother. I'd say, "Grandma, the other kids say I'm a Maori girl, a half caste." You have to understand that in the part of Auckland where we lived, as I recall we were probably the most dark skinned family, and the school was made up of white children. So when someone said that to me at school, it was with the intention of making me feel on the outer, less acceptable, and it was completely successful. I felt embarrassed, ashamed and marginalised.

This is how it works wherever imperialism reigns. The suffering of so many First Nations peoples is an abomination. I had no idea of that then, and now I am so grateful David has pursued his course of learning about all of this. I salute his humility and love of culture. His unstoppable efforts to see the treasures of the nations celebrated and brought into the culture of so many 'white' churches. Our music is different now.

Back then I never let on how I felt; instead I bit my nails down to the quick and chewed the edges off the collars of my clothes. I was a misfit. Justice had it that I was good at sports and I had pretty clothes. My grandmother saw to that, even though she was forever mending my chewed collars. She made me new dresses often, not from new fabric; she found most of her stuff at what back in the day were called jumble sales – wealthier people's cast offs. She had learned where to look and how to find her silk, satin, linen and lace.

I was always decked out in something lovely, even down to my feet because one of my uncles owned a business making shoes. He was a generous, wealthy man who let me choose the latest styles. At school it was always assumed that I came from a wealthy family. My father worked on the wharf and my mother did shop work and scrubbed wealthy people's floors so I could learn ballet and my brother could follow his pursuits. They never thought of themselves, they had such big hearts. You couldn't have made me look much better and I couldn't have felt much worse about myself.

One of the good things this experience has gifted me with is the love of culture. I am intrigued and totally delighted to see, for example, a troop of indigenous dancers and musicians – so exquisite. Too bad the little boy at my school grew up dancing the 'white' way when his family had within them all the vibrant colours, clothing and jewellery of exotic India hidden away for fear of rejection. At least to some extent we celebrate that now too. I thank God it's changing. The haka of our Maori warriors was mostly only on the marae, a Korean drum had never been heard in Aotearoa, and no Samoan slap dance or Siva. Sadly I never learned the dances and ways of my Adriatic heritage like so many who came from other lands.

So this question I posed, the same unrelenting question right through my childhood, was like a dripping tap. Always there, always avoided, as my grandmother answered me in such denial because of her own fear of rejection. With all the dismissal of a captain of the armed forces, her reply to my question came back regularly and always the same. I'd say, "They say I'm Maori?". She would say, "Well, they're wrong, our family comes from Scotland". I know now why no one revealed what my lineage was. It never occurred to me to ask where my grandfather came from, he died years before. I had never met him. I had seen a photo of him. In fact at that stage of my life I saw him every night.

My uncles were back from the war, one very fractured from being imprisoned in Germany living basically on scraps of cabbage an old German lady poked through the fence wires occasionally at enormous risk to herself. She said to him, "My son... in prison in England". It's how his body survived; his mind and emotions never really did. All I knew was he sat staring into space, unable to recount to anyone the horrors he experienced; just drinking all day and never talking about what was done to him at that camp. It was simply too painful to discuss and most veterans – our true heroes – were the same back then. Don't ever shun the homeless and those on death row when you don't know their stories.

He was given my bedroom and I slept on the big brown velvet sofa in our 'front room'. The isolation of it and lack of familiarity were scary to me, but not vaguely to the extent of what was above me. On the wall above the sofa was a large photograph of my grandfather. I don't know why but I was afraid of him. He stared right at me so that I always turned the other way. If I'd looked closely at the picture and if I had a way to work it out, it would have been obvious he was my colour, only darker.

After my mother died in 1981, my brother George, who was by this time intrigued about our roots, made a trip to the northern part of our island to a town called Kaeo from where my family came. What he discovered from the documents of births, deaths and marriages was that we had descended from the northern Maori tribes of Ngapuhi and Opouri. It only took a piece of paper to work it out.

I grew up knowing I was different from those around me. I now know all cultures are to be celebrated and respected. At high school there was a small mixture of ethnicities, but I still lived a large part of my life never really knowing or understanding anything much about the branches that had emerged over centuries, sometimes shamefully and silently, from our family tree. Funny thing is family trees have cupboards full of skeletons they wish to hide. I was mostly unaware of the South Pacific Adriatic mix that came to be me – I never knew of the richness created by genetic fusion.

Like a lot of families some of our heritage is clearly documented but some, like I said, is discreetly shoved as a skeleton in the closet. Here's a bit of a look for you. Explorer Kupe at the top of our family tree on my maternal side is from the Big Island of Hawaii, the place I feel most at home. We have ohana (family) there that love us relentlessly as we love them. Why, you might well wonder, had these facts become a subject never to be discussed? As with most family trees, and even in the most holy of books the bible, there are indiscretions that can so easily bring shame to generations of people. Because of that they are often closeted away until someone, like my brother in our case, unearths the truth and solves the mystery. As a historian, his daughter Kathy is always finding out more about our heritage.

Having lived this long I am very acquainted with how vulnerable we humans are and how a decision involving one's moral compass can change a life in a moment of time and reach down the generations. It would be a terrible indictment if a person lived out their whole life believing they were a mistake. I was in a maze of prejudice; how do people become the judge of how we should live and look as different cultures.

I am pretty sure if my brother and I had known the truth, it would have made little difference to how we felt about our forebears. In fact we may have had greater understanding of their struggle to conceal the pain they all bore in different ways. Yet we do what in our humanity we can do, and as great grandparents, grandparents and parents, we always strive to protect our progeny from what we think could hurt them. Watch the scene with 'wisdom' (Sophia) explaining prejudice in the movie "The Shack". That little rhyme 'sticks and stones may break my bones but names will never hurt me' is a most terribly misguided recitation, very far from the truth.

By the time I moved on to intermediate school (junior high), I had in some ways developed a few life skills. But probably in the long run they were inherited, just waiting to be found, as I watched and absorbed how my grandmother chose to do life. Adeline had a way of making all things around her beautiful. I realised a long time ago it was her way of coping with what you could call the 'ugliness' that had visited her real life. She lived with the shame of her own teenage pregnancy and too soon became a widow with no home and no place to call her own. Most of her children's marriages were in various stages of difficulty. She simply found ways to make things bearable, and beauty became her choice, for the most part. To beautify her surroundings eased her pain.

I mentioned her faith, it was rock solid always, but the other thing that defined her was her service to others. I love the saying, "We will preach the gospel and use words if we have to". It's what she did; her hands, her good works and her big heart were her gospel. I never heard her talk about 'having to find herself', she did that by caring for others. Within that ethos is the panacea for most ills. The pleasure she got from taking care of everyone, meant her life that could have otherwise overwhelmed her, seemed to give her a certain wondrous satisfaction. As a young person I could see that and I cherish the fact that I was a benefactor of all she made so beautiful.

Never did I hear her recite all she had lost or how hard her life had been and it certainly had. Instead she would say to me, "Get your ballet shoes and put on your tutu (a lovely pink confection she made for me), and we will go to The Happiness Club." It was a place for high tea where a lot of lonely women found some solace in each other during and after the war. "When you dance for them," she always claimed, "it will make them forget their troubles, just for a bit."

So steadfast, I'm not sure it occurred to her that not everyone possessed her kind of grit, but she used the same philosophy for herself. No self pity, she just pressed on, and it seemed to me that everything she touched was transformed into something lovely. Both my daughters inherited that gift in different ways: Rachel with her radical style, and Melinda so classic by preference.

Adeline played beautiful music on the radio. She loved orchestral pieces but her favourite was Vera Lynn:

> "We'll meet again
> don't know where
> don't know when
> but I know we'll meet again
> some sunny day".

The truth of it was sheer optimism but it helped people get through the rigour of war time.

She always read the "Women's Weekly" for beauty tips and decor ideas, ever searching for ways to make everyone's life better. To learn and to pass on is what I find is so responsible and so right. There were other tips in those mags as well. You've got to laugh (or cry) because some of the tips back then were things like, "When looking after your man, make sure he can find his wallet". And…"Be sensitive because after a hard day's work, your man needs his slippers right by his chair". Are you kidding me?

She always had a project or two going on that would enhance something or someone's life. One day she and my father brought me some silkworms and showed me how to spin the silk. We watched them eat our mulberry tree to pieces then, as she told it to me, they made cocoons and went to sleep. These orange, yellow, lemon and cream coloured cones with feathery strands were unwound and used to make silken threads for tiny dolls clothes. The dolls were the wooden 'dolly' clothes pegs everyone used on their clotheslines in those days. There was a scarcity of iPhones for entertainment back then, but at least no kids of twelve had 'text neck' with their vertebrae all messed up. It's true and really happening. Tell them to keep their phones at eye level, no kidding, it's a documented condition.

Well some of her magic must have rubbed off on me. By the time I was eleven and at intermediate school I was making my own dresses as she guided me on her old treadle Singer sewing machine. I managed to top the class making a garment that involved intricate smocking. It's so nice to see the royal children are still wearing smocked clothes. I'm glad the art never died completely. I found myself gravitating to all things beautiful, graceful, appealing and glamorous. It's one reason I've chosen to live in an ordered fashion. Mess messes with my head. Order makes everything more beautiful for me. I love to fall into clean, white sheets and I love the cold side of the pillow. Is that crazy?

Melinda is always surrounding me with fragrant flowers in old silver vases I've found at flea markets. It's a simple and at the same time luxurious thing for me. I'm also extremely fortunate that David is so good at bringing me flowers; he always has and I love that he does. When I arrived back home recently from being away writing, he gave me such an enormous bunch of flowers I divided them up into several vases. Freesias, rare white daffodils, fragrant lilies and stock, everything white, everything he knows I love. It's one reason part of my heart tugs towards the tropics, just one fragrant frangipani (plumeria) blossom and you've got me... right there.

Back at intermediate school there was a ritual that happened when I was in my first year. On Friday afternoons the teacher would head to the black board. She was ruthless, straight to the point and up went weekly test results for what was called arithmetic. Anything with numbers and I froze solid. Fifty percent off is the only mathematical equation I understand, pretty much to this day. She did a kind of graph of our twenty two names in a line down the board and then each day's scores. The best you could hope for in a week was fifty: ten out of ten each day. My unbroken record never changed much – a good score got me between ten and twenty marks for the entire week. Obviously I always had, without fail, the lowest score. It was something everybody joked about.

I was the one who had to stay back to be told, among other things, I would never amount to anything if I didn't concentrate, I'd never make it, as if I didn't know. However... I was often the one who had some cute boy waiting to walk me home from school. It made little difference to me that I actually came top in home science. It was viewed as the class for dummies where you learned to sew and cook basics. I could read a recipe and had the kindest teacher. Nothing consoled me though, even first prize for needlework that was very intricate, because academically, and the way things were taught back then, it reinforced in me that I was a non achiever.

I didn't have to see it on a black board either because the teacher went out of her way to expose the few of us who were 'just not trying'. It was like her mission to make struggling students feel bad. I understand her attitude now, I've encountered it in other walks of life and I feel sad for her and all others like her. I've come to know, and specialists in human behaviour have confirmed it, that people who get satisfaction from making others feel bad and diminished are those who essentially feel bad about themselves.

Very often I've noticed too that this way of admonition can stem from a certain guilt such people tend to carry within themselves and go on to blame other people for their ruined lives. Maya Angelou said, "It's important to know in life that when people tell you, especially in anger, how bad you are, they are always talking about themselves." If you have never read her book "I know Why The Caged Bird Sings", it's a revelation. Unable to speak for seven years after being raped, this dignified African American woman became a hero. An accomplished poet as well, she recited one of her poems at a presidential inauguration. Please read anything she wrote that you can get your hands on.

I was trapped in the dread that I would never learn the important stuff or be smart, and I let that incubate inside my head. No matter how good I was at anything, by the time I had finished school I had developed an unfounded bad self image. I told myself what school had told me; I was a dumb half caste.

The fact is our brains, as you may be aware but it bears repeating anyway, are malleable. Negative thinking definitely (it's a proven fact) reinforces negative neurological pathways. The opposite is true as well. Positive thinking, hope, optimism, faith, belief in a God who cares for us and about us: these factors enforce our neurological pathways positively, so the outcome results in joy — that deep down salve. How much I needed to know what we know now: that our mind can tell us repetitive lies and our mouths can so quickly reinforce them.

Don't confuse joy with happiness. Joy is knowing all will be well, happiness, well... it all depends... At least I know this now but as I reached my teens, on one hand I had living proof that I had the ability to achieve on some levels. I had medals for gymnastics. Sometimes I even created a win for the basketball team just by shooting enough goals to put points on the board. I came top of my class for over ten years in all my ballet exams. But on the other hand none of this spoke to me of what real intelligence was and I chose to let myself feel marginalised.

Now I know but then few people understood. No one I came across ever taught about the fact that thoughts – and even more particularly words – are really the creation of the human mind. We are not our mind. We have the capacity to choose both our thoughts and our words. Our brain kicks in to what our mind is telling it and makes it happen either way. Martha Beck, one of the most interesting women I've read, is very enlightening and helpful. She is always encouraging people to process and think in lateral ways that have been very beneficial to me. One thing she says that has stuck with me is this:

> "We basically experience the world we 'think' into being."

Our thoughts, our imaginations and our ruminations can so often lay a trap for us, partly because we can so easily get into comparisons and that suffocates our very own uniqueness. It's not news that there are no two of us the same. We all know the mindboggling finger print thing: the DNA that sets us apart from every other human being.

I guess for so many years I saw my own identity as an embarrassment instead of any kind of asset. The sad thing about that is it meant I wasn't really aware of two things. Firstly, yes I am uniquely created. Secondly, I can change my thoughts, which means I'm not stuck in the dilemma of negative thinking. So now each day when I wake my first words, whether out loud or just in my mind, are those of thankfulness and optimism. It is a habit I have persevered with. For me it took some practice, but I find it's a navigational tool for what is coming during any given day. I can actually choose what I want to think.

My understanding of neuroscience has changed everything. I've found that my feelings and my behaviours are basically influenced irrevocably by the words I use. The change wasn't an overnight thing but eventually I found myself waking up saying, "I take your grace, my Father, thank you. I know it will be sufficient to see me through today". For example it can be teaming with rain but I won't say 'what a bad day'. Who wants to be trapped in a bad day? So those kinds of statements are how I mostly wake up. To think it could have been that way all along.

Here's a version of Psalm 139 I wrote as lyrics for a song:

"You can see me in the dark
For everything is light to you
You hear me when I'm miles away
While in my heart I long to stay
Though morning wings would take me on
Still you will find me, lead me home.
You know my thoughts
You know everything about me
And every moment
For you know my ways
My life was written down
You planned my destiny
I surrender
Captivated by your love.
Though morning wings would take me on
Still you will find me, lead me home,
For everything there is of me

You knew before I came to be
Within my heart I always knew
That I was born to be with you."
©2006 New Sound Publishing

It's from our album "Coming Home". If you haven't heard it you will find the magnificent live orchestra under the baton of our dearest Fletch Wiley is breathtaking. www.davidanddalegarratt.com

That line "You know everything about me" obviously includes what I now know is my brilliant brain that will actually do what it's told and go about rearranging the circumstances of my mind and then my body's response. Who knew! It's proven knowledge now that we are in fact not necessarily victims of our biology of even our genes, our DNA or our circumstances. My dad died of heart disease at around seventy. He ate wrong foods and he said he only had 'three score years and ten'. He got what he said. So sad. I changed my diet so my DNA changed as well. No heart disease. All his family had it and some died even younger. Our thought patterns and speech, what we do with our circumstances, can redefine us.

This is true of Viktor Frankl, that great hero of Auschwitz. Here is that seriously noble quote of his.

"We who lived in the concentration camps
remember those who walked through the huts,
comforting others and giving away
their last piece of bread. They were
few in number but they offer sufficient
proof that everything can be taken from
us but one last thing: the last of human

> freedoms – to choose one's attitude
> in any given set of circumstances,
> to choose one's own way."

He put it another way as well when he wrote,

> "Forces beyond our control can take away
> everything you possess, except one thing,
> your freedom to choose how you will
> respond to your situation."

The last of human freedoms in the end then turns out to be what we actually choose to think. It's what we do with our minds and what we do with our speech. Going into my eighth decade I'm still learning it. Dr Caroline Leaf, says: "Every morning when you wake up, new baby brain cells have been born while you were sleeping, that are at your disposal to be used in tearing down toxic thoughts and rebuilding healthy thoughts. The birth of these new brain cells is called neurogenesis."

It's interesting, kind of amusing, that science is finally catching up with the bible, "The mercies of God are new every morning".

Grandma always said, "Sleep makes you smarter". Makes me ponder about how to get those ones with the cell phones to realise that if they could just turn them off and get some sleep, they might get the good grades they were hoping for. I go to sleep in peace, because Jesus said, "My peace I give to you". That's a gift we do well to accept.

Chapter 6

I bring to you my memory maker.."

Amelia

Some things have within themselves the seeds of their own solutions. What I'm about to tell you is one of those things. As I was about to start high school an opportunity presented itself to me that changed my life in so many beneficial and well – delicious – ways...

I was to become part of a tableau that reminds me of that mercurial saying, 'there will always be music'. I became immersed in it in all kinds of ways. I entered into the world of Irving Berlin, yep, he was the Jewish man who paradoxically wrote that song you hear every year, "I'm dreaming of a white Christmas". Christmas? Maybe he couldn't fit Hanukkah into the lyrics, I know how hard it can be! His epic song to me is "God Bless America" and to that I say, amen!

There were George and Ira Gershwin, Cole Porter, Rogers and Hammerstein who, among others, wrote all the show tunes. If you look around at the world of entertainment – arts, music, money – it's a very Jewish scene of chosen people with talent so abundant that we have all benefited from. Some of those songs keep coming back because they are so well crafted.

As a writer of songs I know exactly how necessary it is to make a song memorable. Thank you my dearest Jimmy and Carol Owens for teaching me so much. In my parents' home there was music too, my brother was an accomplished pianist and had his own band. He loved Louis Armstrong, Dave Brubeck, Duke Ellington and many other jazz icons, so did my dad, and I soon learned to love those songs you just had to sing along to. I'll tell you how and why.

I bring to you my marvellous memory maker, the one who created another world for me. A world that had a certain air of refinement and catharsis, and although I never really knew at the time, she would become an irreplaceable mentor and treasure to me. It was a sort of silver lining. She with her own 'je ne sais quoi' gave me a totally other perspective to my life, which at that time seemed pretty commonplace.

Her name was Amelia, my aunt of the aqua topaz eyes and the wheaten gold hair. Still with bronze skin like her siblings, she was a whole other mortal with hair and eyes I longed for. To me she was like a walking revelation of everything dazzling; an elegant, groomed to perfection, wonder. The special kind of presence that belongs only to women who, for want of a better word, have a kind of finesse. A woman who knew how to seek out and engage elegance in everything around her.

She was one who would create for me the most exciting and amazing experiences of my teen years, still so alive in my memory after all this time. I can only describe her as you would a stained glass window. Not entirely because of her outer beauty, for she knew how to make the most of that, but her inner beauty to me was bone china, Stuart crystal, Limoges. Strong enough for most things but breakable when the touch was too firm, yet even when it sadly was, she nearly always mended well.

It's not for me to say anything about that, but we found a very precious solace in each other that gave us both wonderfully sublime ways of escape. Now I know other ways that are rewarding in a whole other way, but back then I didn't know about things like meditation, how to breathe deeply and properly, or how the grace of God was available to me in unlimited supply.

I watched women eye her up discreetly, endeavouring to find out where she got that dress, that bag, those gloves. She exuded a certain mystery, the kind that comes from knowing how to put oneself together. She wore mascara; I'm sure Cleopatra and Queen Esther did too but no one around me did then. Men seemed to swoon over her, especially those in uniform. America was still protecting us well after the war.

She had married a man of considerable means and connections whose family virtually owned the horseracing scene. He was generous with his money and had the latest everything. I stayed with them often, mostly during the week. She was always there after high school, waiting to tell me of a show in town or a movie we had to see. It was a very different home to my parents' place, where my tireless mother was the consummate housekeeper caring for her home to perfection when she wasn't working. In Amelia's home there was chaos and harmony and they seemed to like it that way.

Around the same time my grandmother had moved in to take care of my aunt's house, doing all the cooking, laundry and it seemed to me pretty much everything, including raising the two young children. I watched her train them: "If you drop it, pick it up". Amelia and her husband's guests came and went, and I learned about fish knives, cake forks and fine china. Yet she always ate her seafood right out of the shell, letting some of her Ngapuhi heritage briefly surface. However she only used elegant china plates and her embossed silverware.

She kind of took me in, but never in a way that made me feel like an obligation, only a treasure. We were soul mates, a perfect fit. A mirror of each other. A soul mate, I now realise, is the person who shows you everything that is holding you back; the person who brings you to your own attention so you can enrich your life. That is what she was to me.

Thinking about her now, all those years ago she came to the city with her mother and siblings, hardly any education, and began working in a factory making men's ties. All through her life she educated herself and she never stopped learning. She modelled for me a curiosity for the same thing: to know what is happening, to try to stay informed, to see the bigger picture.

Now I read each night with the dictionary on my phone beside me – the meanings of words I don't know are so easy to access. Like everyone I google everything – how Amelia would have loved all this stuff that has made learning so accessible. As I write I'm seventy nine but the learning side of me is still thriving. YouTube, Ted Talks, Super Soul Sunday (thank you Oprah), anything to keep me informed and satisfy my curiosity. So many books.

She had her mother's kind of optimism. If everything wasn't all right she would do her utmost to make it so – she was the original victura (that is Latin for 'about to conquer'). Optimism does that I've learned, it's hope on wheels. Our body's pharmacy is always open, and hope and expectation are the creators of optimism.

I had learned to manoeuvre heels by the time I was fourteen. She taught me to ballroom dance. We waltzed, we tangoed, we did the fox trot to "Blue Hawaii", as Bing Crosby crooned it out and Elvis did as well. Hawaii, I thought, sounds nice, where was it I wondered? Who knew I'd be right there in Kona off and on for about forty years in my later life.

It was the time of "Show Boat", "South Pacific", "Singing in the Rain". Dancers like Fred Astaire mesmerised me, so did Gene Kelly, then there was Esther Williams who made a swimming pool look like a dance floor. The wonder and anticipation of it all was healing for me. I never knew what she was planning next but it was always enlightening, enriching and fascinating.

Each week she and I went to The Capitol movie theatre and ate a whole big block of Cadbury's chocolate as we vicariously entered another world of make believe from Hollywood. In my later teens I started going to the Wednesday and Saturday night dances at The Crystal Palace and a ballroom called the Peter Pan.

I could dance again but my knee would never sustain me on toe shoes, so ballet was no longer an option. What had happened was so heartbreaking for me. I was attending the Nettleton-Edwards School of Ballet in Auckland studying to become a ballet teacher, the credentials for which came from the Royal Academy of Dance in London. One day as I was demonstrating a sequence of steps for the class, my left knee gave out under me and I crashed to the floor. It was Amelia who rushed me to the emergency room at the local hospital. They said I was young and would mend, then sent me away bandaged, telling me to stay off that leg.

If I'd had the correct treatment at the time I'm pretty sure my knee would have mended properly. (But guess what, in my old life I got a new one!) I ruminated and feared, but it never got completely better, nor would I go to London to dance at Sadlers Wells, which was my dream. There was another course for me, although I was so bereft at the time. Such a great sadness when a dream dies. At least eventually I became fully mobile and I didn't need toe shoes to do the fox trot or waltz anyway… I had regrouped.

It's easier now I fully trust God, although I confess some of the traumas I have encountered have taken time in the regrouping, especially when you are lied about and slandered. Such treatment comes with the territory of those who forge new paths. So exciting.

The dances I went to in those days were very proper. A marvellously decked out Glen Miller style big band played while girls in their frothy skirts, cute little blouses, diamantes and pearls sat waiting to be asked to dance. When it was over one or two boys would always walk me home, where they thanked me, shook my hand and thanked my aunt or grandmother, one of whom always came to the door. I suppose just in case some poor 'wretched boy' (well that was how Grandma thought of them!) tried to steal a goodnight kiss!

Amelia taught me to drive. Although I nearly wrecked the big Humber Super Snipe (it wasn't automatic), thanks to her now driving the freeways of Los Angeles is a breeze – just point me to the 405 or the 101. She also taught me to swim. She couldn't put her head under water because of her mascara. Waterproof makeup hadn't been heard of so of course I learned to swim the same way – head above the water – and have been the object of much mockery from certain sources, well my daughters actually! Tragic but, hey, I never drowned.

She often took me to a place that held me in awe, just from its sheer architectural beauty and plush furnishings – velvet, brocade, golden tassels on drapes and opera boxes from where the classier people would watch the performance. It was (until the city fathers tore it down – progress they said) His Majesty's Theatre. All the best ballet and musical theatre was performed there. We never missed a show, an opera or a ballet.

We would absolutely always dress up. She wore her silver fox furs and I always found something lovely to wear that Grandma or I had made. Often my father would meet us to see a show. A dapper, very gentle gentleman who loved music and dance, he always wore his fedora and his one good jacket and pants with the perfect knife pleat down the front he pressed himself. Amelia's husband never left his club until about ten at night, sometimes bringing home with him the bounty of his wins from a raffle and whatever else he did. Unless they were entertaining together, they both had separate lives.

I marvelled at such talent that came to our city, it was the stuff of dreams for me. My favourite was and always has been the white ballet Swan Lake. Classical and exacting, it challenged me to do well in my own ballet exams and always seemed like my future before I fell.

I remember when Amelia first got a TV. There were two cooking shows she loved: Julia Child and The Galloping Gourmet, Graham Kerr. If I'd known then that one day way in the future the debonair Galloping Gourmet himself and his wife Treena would be house guests with us for a month, I would never have believed it.

Cooking for Graham was something I got to love because he and Treena had a way of celebrating life that was so infectious, you just forgot about being terrified to cook for such a famous chef. He filmed some of his TV series in our kitchen and wanted to look naturally tanned so he used spray tan and ended up filming the series with an orange face and arms! I remember us all roaring with laughter, including Graham. One evening Melinda was making a hollandaise sauce and just as she brought it to the table it separated. He waved his hand in the air and said with all his infectious charm, "Oh just throw an ice cube in it darling, it'll come back together", and it did. He was a Masterchef before the term was invented.

His beloved Treena suffered a heart attack not long after that time. He adjusted his far too lavish recipes, providing her and many of us with a healthier lifestyle. As a result I learned from him and others (I research everything) and ended up losing forty pounds over six months. Happily, I never found them again, not that I'm looking for them. It's true we are what we eat. We will talk more about it. Graham has written some very important books on the subject of eating well. Google him, he is a wealth of information especially if heart disease is in your family. Remember education is power. His Treena, that larger than life woman and talented poet, passed away in 2015. She was dearly loved by so many of us.

Amelia had what one would now call her own worldview. She knew what was happening in the broader sense and was very fixed regarding her feelings about women and equality. The inequality of wages was something she often commented on in terms of women's rights. It goes too far for me on the issue of women's rights when a living baby, still in the womb, has no rights as a human being. Just saying.

I've always been blessed to be around women who challenge the status quo and have their own broad and encompassing perspectives. I learn so much from them. They inspire me as I watch some of them come and go around the world and give back in developing nations. They show me the big picture, one I can't be involved with practically, but I hold many of them in my prayers and contribute wherever I can. If you can't go, give, if you can't give, pray.

It's becoming easier in this millennium for women in some parts of the western world to break free and reach their own potential. In developing nations some amazing things are happening. I've always been an advocate of the ability women have to challenge injustice. If you don't know of Dr Catherine Hamlin, google her. An Australian OB-GYN (obstetrician-gynaecologist) married to a New Zealander. She will completely inspire you. Everyone should see the documentary about her work in Ethiopia, "A Walk To Beautiful". Dr Hamlin is still doing fistula surgeries and she's well over ninety now. She cares for shunned African women in Addis Ababa, many really just young girls. If you have never thought of getting involved with some of these causes run largely by women, I'll note them in the back of the book.

Well... back to Amelia, her thirst for knowledge and self improvement in my orbit was so unusual back then. She listened to a programme on the radio that later became a TV show. It was called, "It's in the Bag" with Selwyn Toogood. Much later it would be hosted by the pro-broadcaster John Hawkesby. A kind and generous man our family has come to love and admire greatly, both he and his family are a gift to us. His daughter, the loyal and lovely Kate, so adeptly and sensitively conducted our Rachel's funeral. My aunt never missed that programme, and amazingly hardly ever missed an answer. They were general knowledge questions and I never knew how she figured the answers. She just said to me, "Books, newspapers, the radio – find out about life".

The reason I told you that is because over my life I too have found it very beneficial to read widely. It's trivial to have a conversation about the weather when there is so much to talk about that matters. I've learned from books as a way to challenge and broaden my thinking, it's how I get incredible inspiration.

I find myself in another life, another place, with botanists on board as they travel the Pacific with Captain Cook, planting, removing, documenting species. I could be going down the Seine River in France with the Eiffel Tower in the background, in Assisi with St Francis, Calcutta with Mother Teresa, or just chilling out with Brennan Manning engrossed in his book "Abba's Child". I have to admit I can be close to heaven, or so it seems, watching Andrea

Bocelli singing in Portofino on YouTube, or learning amazing things when Netflix gives me "Chef's Table".

Yet I always go back to books to read a Psalm like this rendition of Psalm 23 brought to us by Eugene Peterson, a poet in his own right:

> "God, my shepherd!
> I don't need a thing.
> You have bedded me down in lush meadows,
> You find me quiet pools to drink from.
> True to your word, you let me catch my breath
> and send me in the right direction.
> Even when the way goes through death valley
> I'm not afraid when you walk at my side.
> Your trusty shepherd's crook makes me feel secure.
> You serve me a six-course dinner right in front of my
> enemies.
> You revive my drooping head;
> my cup brims with blessing.
> Your beauty and love chases after me
> every day of my life.
> I'm back home in the house of God."

That's pure restoration and hope, as my cup runs over.

I don't know TV shows well because I prefer to read, but then if George Clooney walked across the screen who knows, I could be glued to the set as I would be if Mr Darcy appeared. Then there's Bradley Cooper – one could go on. But to learn and be engrossed in a great book is one of my grand passions.

So for Amelia, learning for her was counterpoint to what else was going on in her life at the time, just like everything of beauty was for my grandmother. Amelia knew suffering but developed ways of tempering it. I watched her make choices. We all do what we can do, we find ways to do life, the ones that work best for us.

No one took antidepressants or anything resembling them back then, not on a regular basis. I've come to learn over many years not to judge how people cope with things they find hard to live with. I know now from research how dangerous and addictive much medicine can be. And how beneficial food, herbs and spices are as medicine. I grow them especially to keep our family well. I would say I believe in many ways to fix things – prayers and petitions absolutely always – and I try to make gratitude a regular go to position. Yet no one really knows another's pain and I acquiesce towards real food, meditation and, where essential, medication. To quote Martha Beck, "Just stay away from those horse tranquillisers!"

Amelia made the best of everything, always planning vacations, mostly to the ocean where we harvested our own seafood from right in front of their place on the beach. We would literally slurp down white bread and butter sandwiches, bursting with succulent steaming tua tua, pipis and fat mussels right off the rocks of the bay. No white bread for me now I've found out gluten is not my friend, but zuppa di vongole al pomodoro – I could jump right into a pot of the stuff!! It's my heritage after all. Another peasant dish, simply clams in an exquisite tomato soup.

They took me to fine hotels where there were printed menus 'du jour'. Three courses served on white plates, white linens and of course silver service. I learned there was a 'right' way to eat soup, but that depends on your culture doesn't it? Of course we all do it differently, there's no 'right way'. In her home you never slouched at the table, talked with food in your mouth or ate with your mouth open. The grandness of the civility of that culture lingers with me.

I always lay the table in a way that's proper for me. I have collected my own silver pieces from garage sales, markets and old stores full of someone else's stuff and I wonder about the stories these objects carry with them. I own a silver tea and coffee service I bought at a second hand shop crowded with forgotten silver pieces from other people's lives. I had the initials DDG and the Latin words of the Garratt crest 'crete crus salus' (sure salvation through the cross) inscribed on each piece so I would have something to hand down for posterity.

So this rite of passage at the bequest of my dearest aunt is so richly memorable to me. It got me through my high school years. I would never have known then, but in later years Amelia's legacy was continued in other ways for me, particularly by two amazing women among several others who were once again to change my life. These two are how I described my Aunt Amelia; soul mates just as she was.

One was my beautiful Babs, who in her gentleness and generosity of spirit extended my observance of all things beautiful to a whole other level with her deep understanding of how to acknowledge the wonder of everything around her. She often recited to me that lovely poem written by thirteenth century poet Muslihuddin Sadi, and I quote:

"If of thy goods thou art bereft
and from thy slender store
two loaves alone are left
sell one and with the dole
buy hyacinths to feed the soul."

You can imagine how a new world opened up yet again as we lived, loved and laughed together about so many things. I learnt from her about grooming, things I'd never known. She has beautiful delicate hands and took the time to show me how to care for mine as well. Then there were her small observations, "Darling your Earl Grey tea tastes much better out of a bone china tea cup with a slice of lemon". Of course I rushed out and found an elegant cup at a market. It was a time in my life, a passage where another kind of refinement was bestowed on me. Now in her eighth decade she is to me more charming than ever. She makes me feel loved to the very depths of my soul.

When I was around fifty I encountered the gift of someone very extraordinary Amelia would have so loved. Her name is Stephanie. Although younger than me she has mentored me with her superb knowledge. She has taught me on so many levels as Amelia did, how to enquire, to learn and truly seize the day in a way only she does. It's hard for me to describe her to you except to say if I ever needed someone to be there for me, there are few in my life as loyal and dependable as this one.

She freely shares all her knowhow about so many things, and carefully shows me everything that can ever enhance my life. For instance she's aware how much I cherish all things silver. She seeks out for me special silver pieces nestled in velvet and silk in their original antique boxes which are almost as beautiful to me as the silver itself. It was she who introduced me to Ralph Lauren and India Hicks, some of the great designers who enhance your home. She taught me you need some silver and crystal to beautify your surroundings, so now I have my own pre-owned statements around the place. It's just of course for the beauty of it.

There are others you'll meet in our Owner's Manuals, people

who are incredibly inspiring as well, but woman to woman she has been my confidante and my teacher in countless unique ways. I have found people like these two have brought such wealth into my life.

I want to encourage you that when you come across those who inspire you and you take from them their treasures, always look for ways to contribute to them as well. I mention these two because of the way they have continued Amelia's legacy for me. It would be impossible for me to begin to name the many men and women who have gifted me with all kinds of knowledge and inspiration over the years to whom I'm profoundly grateful. One of a kind people all freely loving and giving me different and marvellous perceptions out of their beautiful hearts.

I had no idea there would be another course for me, but it would not be long before someone else turned up in my life. I was just twenty when I met him. Tall, dark and of course handsome, his name was David. Yes he had freckles and he was another one of those with the clear, topaz green eyes that would one day stare back at me through our daughter Rachel. He worked out at the gym so the overall visual had its own appeal. Still does.

That nearly sixty year journey was about to begin and who knows when it will end, but if anything was engineered or as they say 'ordained by God', well he and I are one of those stories. Before I go there I want to show you some of the things of value to me that have enabled me to partner this man, at least to a better degree than I might have if I had not had the personal experience of knowing God's love for me. It became a true reality when I was about twenty and in turn started me on a long journey that seems so short now. Every human being is born with the certain tragic dilemma; they have to grow up.

I mention valuables, well they're not always quantifiable but you know when you own them; whether you wear them, display them, use them, or if they are what becomes part of you. At the time when I made a very conscious, clear-cut choice to become a Christian, it was never as though I didn't have any idea of what that meant, but how could I know it was my most valuable life decision.

At the age of fourteen, after my grandmother had taken me to church each Sunday throughout my childhood, I knew the ropes, it was a bible believing Church of Christ. The night I decided to respond to the preacher's invitation to follow the Christian faith, I did so because I wanted to please my grandmother, my brother entering into the ministry, and the very pretty minister's wife. I didn't really understand one very fundamental thing about doing this though, because quite obviously at that moment in my life it was for my own gain for all the wrong reasons.

Now I know the right reason and it will never be anything other than the fact of personally encountering the Triune God. Church always said to me you must come to God. It never occurred to me that in fact God had made me for friendship with him. God said to me it's me who needs you. To me it's a mystery that can't be fathomed in any intellectual way: you either believe it to be true or you don't. It's a faith thing. I've come to the conclusion that we are in fact spirits having a human experience, or else nothing makes sense to me. Someone said our body is like the rental car we drop off at the airport and then when we take the plane it's our spirit, the real us, that departs from our body.

When I was about eighteen and finishing an apprenticeship as a dressmaker of beautiful ball gowns, I was saving money for an overseas trip. Through my aunt I had met many Americans protecting New Zealand as allies during and for some time after the war. The American Navy was a familiar sight. They seemed to gravitate to the beautiful Amelia. I liked them; they were friendly, positive, generous people and because of that it was my intention to go to the USA one day soon.

I was saving my money working two jobs, one was at a cafe where a guy started to come in regularly. He had a kind of American accent, he had the clothes, the look. I didn't know, but he had been to a bible college in California. I would overhear him talking as he had his coffee and the best mud pie made of pure chocolate my boss was known for around town. I want it now! Well, maybe not! I was a bit smitten by him – when I wasn't thinking about Elvis Presley (whom I was sure to meet in America, I had no doubt). How intriguing fate is. Who knew we were destined to record an album way in the future with some of Elvis Presley's band members?

When the guy came to the cafe one Friday afternoon and sat at a table, I worked that area of the room relentlessly. I had tried in vain to get his attention before but he always had friends with him. I later learned he brought them off the street and offered them coffee as a way of doing his evangelism.

I had asked if I could start work early because I was going to a dance with a bunch of friends around eight o'clock that night. I would change into my dress at the cafe and take the tram up Queen Street to the Peter Pan. You could go most places by yourself in those days. As I was walking out the door dressed in pink moiré French taffeta pinched in at the waist – a full frothy skirt covered in white flocking hailstone dots – just as I began to put on my coat he stood to his feet and looked me in the eye. I think I all but passed out and then he asked me if I was free tomorrow. After making a polite introduction, he said he could pick me up at five thirty. I was so stunned by his question that no matter what I had been going to do tomorrow, it would have been of no consequence.

I probably stammered out that I was free at that time. He asked where I lived, "803 Mt Eden Road", I said, then he asked something like was I going dancing and I told him I was and where. Before I left he called to me and said, "See you at five thirty tomorrow… morning". What?! Wait a minute, who went anywhere on a date at five thirty in the morning? He clarified that quickly by saying he was taking me to a prayer meeting. I was stunned and at the same time too smitten by him to refuse.

After the ball my girlfriend's father drove me home in the early hours of Saturday, scolding us both for keeping him waiting so long. All I could think was what do I wear? What's appropriate, what do you have to do at a prayer meeting? White, I decided on white, it had the angelic feel that would make me fit right in. How was I to know that no one else would be wearing a tight white sweater and very well fitting pants? It was the days of Marilyn Monroe and everything was two sizes too small.

I was mortified, no one wore makeup, not because they didn't believe in it but who would bother at that time of the morning? Every time I moved my head my long dangly earrings rattled – talk about 'this thing has disaster written all over it'. I looked around the room and everyone had big black bibles. I felt so horribly out of place, but they were all so welcoming and kind and there was no rock to crawl under so there was only one thing for it. Having been a dancer it was easy for me to recall my performance skills because for many years I'd been on stage. I could pretend – I did this regularly, it would be a breeze.

Over the hour or so that followed I was to be enlightened about what it was like to truly know God. They all chatted with him as if he was in the room. How could you do that? They did and they thanked him often because he had answered their prayers that week. I never let on but I was dumbfounded to think you could actually converse with God in such an intimate way. My reference points became skewed because I had never understood I could relate to a God like that. In fact I think my secret belief was if I didn't behave and do good he might stamp me out like an ant. It's taken me the rest of my life so far to engage with the enormity of the love, grace and mercy of God. Please read Paul Young's book, "Lies We Believe About God." So much to learn.

There are three amazing stories in the Gospel of Luke, chapter 15. It is Jesus Christ telling these parables – the three in a way are really one. One is about a woman who frantically searched everywhere for a coin she lost, and about her huge relief and unbridled joy when she found it after scouring the whole house clean. After all it's usually only a woman who takes the time to scour and search in my experience anyway. When she found her valuable coin she threw a party.

Another of the three stories is of a boy old enough to leave home who demands his inheritance to go his own way. He messed up badly and finally thought, I'll just have to go back to my father and maybe he will take me on as one of his servants. Turns out his father had been watching and waiting, looking out onto the horizon each day for a glimpse of that boy he loved so dearly. He watched, waited, longed and yearned for his boy. Well the boy finally arrived home, broken and humbled with a speech prepared about how unworthy he was to be called a son. Before he could complete his speech his father, so the story goes, was kissing that son of his and holding him close. He had come home where he belonged. His father's longing was fulfilled and he threw a party.

The story I love best of these three is called "the lost sheep". It is Jesus talking, I quote: "If you have one hundred sheep and one of them strayed away and was lost in the wilderness, wouldn't you leave the ninety nine others to go and search for the lost one until you found it? And when you found it you would, with such joy, carry it home on your shoulders." The pathos of that scene undoes me! Jesus turned to the crowd and said, "Wouldn't you find everyone you knew around there and throw a party?"

I can only say, to be placed on the shoulders of that shepherd because he was searching for me is utterly breathtaking. George MacDonald made this profound statement:

> "This has been the Father's work from the beginning, to bring us into the home of his heart, this is our destiny."

That day in that room I was a lost coin, I was a lost and mindless teenager like that boy, and I was a lost lamb in the wilderness. I was all three. I was lost and found within the space of an hour. My life was before and after I met a God who actually wanted me; he longed for my company. I had always thought it was about me needing him and yet to think he actually needed me.

It couldn't have been more different, I just didn't know a God in three persons, the Trinity. A father, a redeemer and a paraclete – the helper, deliverer and comforter – that truly feminine aspect of God in whose image we are made. Right at the beginning God was walking in the garden in the cool of the evening and he called, "Adam, where are you?" I know now this God who found me is the God who is out looking, searching, waiting, and in one moment we can be within the home of his heart.

There's something I came to figure out about these three stories told in the Gospel of Luke. So subtle really, I missed it for a long time. It's an aside to these stories that may interest you. I've discussed it with people who know theology and no one has disagreed with me yet, although it's not something I had considered until a few years ago.

God, right from the beginning, presented his personhood as three in one, and these stories Jesus told are a perfect picture of this Triune God. There is a father, a good shepherd (which is how Jesus described himself) and then there is a woman searching so desperately as well. A father, son and a feminine figure. I find these three parables to be where Jesus gives us a heads up. I think he's giving us a look at the Trinity in a very lovely way. He sometimes qualifies his stories by saying, "Those who have ears to hear, let them hear". I'll explain how I understand (hear) these parables.

Way back in the first book of the bible, Genesis chapter 1, it says, "So God created human beings, in his own image he created them, male and female". One of the Hebrew names of God is El-Shaddai. The word Shaddai comes from the root word 'breast'. Literally translated it would mean 'the many breasted one'; not a masculine image.

Another interesting factor in my reasoning about this reference to the Trinity in Luke chapter 15, is that back in the book of Genesis when God created the woman he said she would be a "helper". That word is in fact the same word in the Greek translation that is used in scripture to describe the Holy Spirit, the counsellor, the deliverer, the comforter, the helper.

I'm no theologian myself so I can't really say more than that in God's search for us it looks to me very much like the three persons of the Godhead are doing the searching. It makes sense to me that they are male and female in his own image, so it stands to reason that one part of the Trinity is feminine and I deem that part to be the Holy Spirit, the helper, the comforter. It is in fact the description of Eve of whom God said, "I will make a helper", and he chose to create her as a woman. So although people mostly refer to the Holy Spirit as 'he', I propose 'she' may be the appropriate pronoun.

Presuming we all took a deep breath and those of us who have decided to go for the long haul with me are still here, I will do my best to tell you the story of 'us': David, me and our daughters.

Remembering

SCRIPTURE IN SONG
Let us c
thanksg
And ex
For the t
God
The grea
GOODIES
INSIDE
YARD
SALE

Chapter 7

"I knew I would remember
the scent of those flowers
forever and always think of him…"

DG and Me

Last night when we were having dinner with our superb neighbours Anthea and Tani, they said someone had remarked, "You know the Garratts? They're famous". Well here's the inside scoop. If you don't know you can't do something, the possibilities are endless.

We were young and very zealous about our faith. I'm thinking we knew nothing too much about life, but if we had to, if I had to, I would still do it all again with David, this kind of eccentric man whom I often think is more of a spirit being than a human being. An unquantifiable, totally unpretentious person who is definitely endearing.

Here's a piece he wrote in his journal in 1992. "I walked home from work last night and thought I should climb Mt Hobson and listen to the Lord. I sat near the top on the side of the hill facing the ocean. A large pine tree was in front of me. Its trunk divided at about nine feet. The two trunks grew side by side for another fifteen feet, then both sprouted branches and both produced an equal amount of fruit (cones). One of the trunks was larger than the other.

It seemed to me as if this tree represented Dale and me. I was the trunk on the ocean side to offer support to Dale. When the branches reached twenty four feet, the larger one backed off a little to allow the other one to continue growing straight. Both had some damaged branches that didn't seem to intertwine much at the branch level but rather develop together side by side.

It seemed like it spoke of Dale and me, and that we were about at the stage of beginning to sprout. Probably the fruit was going to be the release of various people; different groups for both of us but equally as productive as the other. The ocean side trunk was on a cliff face and desperately needed to keep gripping the earth, just as I needed to trust in God for us both."

This metaphor of David's has proven to be true throughout our union. Since our 'I do' we have been interdependent: the best and most workable form of relationship you can ever hope for. Here's how it had its beginnings. I remember it like you remember all precious memories.

It was an evening in spring. It had to be springtime; it was one of those unusually warm September nights. We had just met a few months before when he was on stage with one of his seven sisters, a sweetheart named Janice, he was playing guitar and they were both singing. I was just a person in the audience but later he confessed to having noticed me. I was never sure whether it was me he noticed or if it was the hat I was wearing. We need to clear that up some time!

Back on that September night as we walked up the stairs to our friends' house, the air was still and scented with the perfume of Indian jasmine – a fusion of musk, mangoes, vanilla and honey. A huge old vine was rambling up the railing to the door, a pungency of such sweetness was suspended in a cloud of white blossoms. It was something you wanted to capture somehow so it would stay with you forever. Sensuous in all the right ways. I happened to look up and as is always the case on a clear Antipodean night, the Southern Cross hung there in a galaxy of stars, bold and beautiful.

Out of the blue David snapped off a branch of jasmine and without a word just handed it to me and then wandered off inside.

I knew I would remember the scent of those flowers forever and always think of him. We had no way of knowing how the following years and decades would unfold, the things we would do, the rewards, the cost, the privilege and the price. It has always been enough for us that God knew and had a plan. The alchemy of it is still unfolding as it always has, but the undeniable history of it has been deeply humbling and outweighs all else.

We were there that night to rehearse with our friends who we sang with. Soon after that they had a child and then there were two: David and me. We were entirely focused on recording weekly radio programmes that were broadcast to missionaries. We sang at all sorts of youth events and for some reason we became a popular duo and were asked to appear all around town. We took our preparation for these things very seriously – we would pray together and work on our songs. When I look back we were anything but professional yet everything about earnest.

One day after about two years of this, we drove out into the countryside to prepare for an event. David has always had a passion for the land, he wanted to go farming when he left school and even did so for a couple of years. So off we went, guitar and bibles, always interested in hearing what God wanted to tell us.

There was a sluggish stream meandering along just below a meadow where we sat down. We often picked berries or wild flowers – I couldn't help myself – but this day we just sat listening to the cicadas, the rustling trees, and the gurgle of the stream as it was reflected in a cloudless blue Pacific sky. The smell of wild mint and other grasses was delectable.

We were together preparing for an event so David opened his bible, as he often did, to read a psalm or some scripture. How could we have known that the piece he randomly read would be such consequential words for us, written way back by the prophet Isaiah. Those verses would become our mandate and our life's work together. Here is what we read from the book of Isaiah in chapter 49:

> "Listen to me all you distant islands,
> pay attention you who are far away...
> at just the right time I will respond to you, I will help you."

It went on to say many things, words that would become our destiny together. It was a clear message from God to us. We were as far away as possible from where those words were written – indeed in the uttermost part of the earth. Even though we knew innately it was true, we had no understanding of how it would play out over time.

David had been staying with a relative of his who had become a spiritual mentor to me. She was a bible teacher and had her own clear mission 'to know God and make him known'. I will be forever grateful that my life has been touched by this petite giant of the Christian faith, Joy Dawson.

A short while before the day we were to read that scripture together, she came to me and told me that as she was combing her hair looking in the mirror, she had an impression of David and me standing behind her. We were together, she explained, because God meant us to be together. It kind of shook me up because before that morning when I truly encountered God for the first time back at the five thirty prayer meeting, I had dated just about everyone in the free world – so to speak – so after that time I made a clear cut decision to wait and never date again until I knew I had found the right person. I wanted to trust God completely about this and do it right. After Joy told me what she felt, I realised I must be open to the possibility that David was that person. I suppose on 'the night of the jasmine' I could have recognised that, but because of my reasoning I never let myself go there.

I'm glad we had two years of ministry together before this because it gave us a chance to learn about each other. We are such very different people from two totally different worlds. It's still a wonder to me how we came to be together and form a relationship with the gravity of staying power we have had from the very beginning. I know opposites attract and all that, but seriously, we were and still are polar opposites.

My family, my upbringing, my one brother nine years older than me had gone off to university before I started high school. I never really knew him except that he was the musical, academic one, with the sensational personality. We never had much time together, but we were destined to become great friends eventually. His latest birthday card to me – so affectionate – made me feel very much loved indeed:

> "To my dear and very much loved sister.
> A very happy birthday... And many more.
> Love from your ancient brother!"

We don't share the same faith, just the same respect and love.

The Garratts were such a different family from mine. David with his ten siblings and a heritage of generation after generation of faith filled Christian men and women. His mother Florence (I cherish every memory of my relationship with her) was one of my all time heroes. Her presence and influence on my life was pivotal.

Her encouragement and affirmation of me was something that brought me the deepest comfort. She was a woman of pure goodness, guilelessness with such a simple, practical faith. That feeling of 'all will be well, darling', always returns to me when I think of her and how she unconditionally accepted me for her precious firstborn son, David.

When he was around four and at preschool, he told me about the day he sang a song about heaven. I can imagine that earnest little freckled face staring at his teacher as he sang:

> "I shall wear a golden crown
> When I get home;
> Clad in robes of glory
> I shall sing the story
> Of the Lord who bought me
> When I get home."

I love that the teacher said to him, "I'm sure you will David".

You can see from my story that our worlds were very different. His mother had seven daughters and four sons of her own. She had lost two others, one stillborn and another, John, who died of meningitis at two years old. Yet her love for our daughters and me is something that could never possibly be replaced in my life. Later I'll tell you what happened with our youngest daughter Rachel, but Mother wept every single time we talked of Rachel's passing, such unbridled grief. It was the same when we spoke of her great grandchildren, Millie and Ihaka. It seemed the loss of their mother was unbearable for her, compounded by the fact that for the final years of her life she was sadly never to see them again. It was a matter entirely out of our control that compounded the pain of her tender heart, and mine and David's as well. I would put her in the Motherhood Hall of Fame in a heartbeat.

So having had Joy tell me how she felt about David and me, I wasn't surprised when a few days after that he called and asked me to go to the beach with him, even though this was never how we had worked together. Our relationship up to this point was always only platonic and focused on what we were doing – singing, recording – those things. It had been that way from the beginning. I agreed to go, I was intrigued! I found out Joy hadn't put him up to it. It was just his capricious nature I guess.

We went in his brand new car that came with his job as a tea taster. Right there I could have got a massive clue about how he rolls, because we got out of the car with the picnic lunch my mother had made us and were about to set it up. Big, fat roast beef sandwiches and lemonade she had made from scratch. It was lamingtons oozing cream and jam for dessert; she had made those as well. Everything looked like the dream day. Black and silver sand, Lion Rock just off shore looking proud and picturesque, the surf crashing headlong onto its base.

Then came the announcement that has been repeated over these decades more times than I care to remember. Did he turn breathless and tell me he had loved me for those two long years? Did he want to tell me that he too had a message from God telling him I was the only one for him? It could have been a moment! Instead this is what he told me, those green eyes looking confused so I guessed he didn't love me, I could deal with that. No it wasn't any of those things. He simply stared at me helplessly and announced, "I've lost the car keys".

We spent a long time searching, tracing our tracks through sand and grasses, and by late afternoon he came running with great jubilation towards me. He had found the keys by the car door. We packed up our things and as we walked back to the car he put an arm around me, and right there was 'a moment'. The thing was, neither Joy nor I had mentioned anything to him about her earlier revelation to me, so as they say, timing is everything.

Although by now David had worked in the city, dressing as a young executive right down to his polished shoes and always wearing a suit and tie, his true heart, as I said before, was still back on the land. He had left home when he was sixteen to learn about farming and I think, in fact I know, if he had been given a choice then he would have wanted to have his own farm with livestock and a big vegetable garden. He doesn't do any kind of sophistication or pretension whatsoever unless the occasion calls for a protocol. He would pony up, as he had to for his job, and I have to say he looks pretty good in black tie as well.

One time not long after we officially became a couple, I mentioned to him that every Christmas I had a tradition of attending a performance of Handel's Messiah. It was one of those events where you absolutely did dress up. There was a live orchestra and the best singers and choir Auckland city could muster. I loved everything about it. To hear en masse scores of voices proclaiming the anthem, "King of kings and Lord of lords forever and ever hallelujah, hallelujah", still gives me chills up my spine. David had never been to any kind of show or performance (not everyone has an Amelia in their life), so we decided we would go together.

It would be an experience he would never forget. I knew how he loved the scriptures and Handel had done a masterful job of crafting together the story of Jesus Christ from the beginnings back when Isaiah so prophetically announced that a child, a son, would be born, on whose shoulders would finally rest the government of the world. He told of how this man would feed his flock like a shepherd and gather us like lambs into his arms to carry us close to his heart. He would be the one to take upon himself all of our broken lives, as he healed us and gifted us with true peace and the wonder of his grace. That's the time to use the adjective 'divine'. Why do people call food or clothing or a vacation divine? Just asking.

These prophecies had always captivated me, especially as time went on. I came to understand that only divine inspiration could have caused a man, thousands of years before, to describe in manifest detail the life, death and resurrection of Jesus Christ our Redeemer. The great aria, "I know that my redeemer liveth and that he shall stand in the latter day upon the earth", to me is the summation of the greatest of all stories. He shall stand because he will return.

I was excited. I made a new dress and I could hardly wait for David to experience an evening of such spell binding culture for himself. Different dates and my father had often given me flowers, but David didn't seem to be the type to bother with such convention. You can imagine my surprise when he arrived, hands behind his back, obviously holding a bunch of something for me. How sweet, how unexpected. Nothing could have prepared me for what happened next. He stood there, a perfect picture of someone who had made an effort. Great suit and tie, hair with the side part of the day. As we Kiwis would say, 'he scrubbed up nicely'.

My mind was doing the anticipation dance! Violets, I thought, they have always been my favourites. Maybe a red rose or a corsage to wear on my dress? The expectation was a thrill in itself. I know I was excited because I remember having to rearrange my facial expression quickly when with some pride and that endearing grin, he produced a bunch of red radishes and thrust them toward me. He had just harvested them straight from a small patch of garden he was cultivating at the place where he had room and board. Guess I wouldn't be wearing those to the Town Hall.

We had the best seats, I'd made sure we were right there in the front. I had danced in recitals on that very stage in my ballet years. We settled into our seats, I can't remember but I'm sure I would have sighed with the pleasure of it all. The lights went down, the orchestra started, "The Messiah" had begun. Half way into the third song I turned, about to ask him, "Are you loving it? Totally? Like me?" He was in a deep sleep. I was so completely amazed that such a thing could be possible, clearly too much gardening… not enough culture, I had no idea what to do. He only woke when everyone rose to their feet for the "Hallelujah Chorus" and he never even looked a bit embarrassed. As I said, no pretence… what you see is what he is.

Over the years I've tried to sneak in a little culture here and there but he has never attended a ballet with me and I wouldn't ask him to. I'd need to bring along a pillow and blanket! I think I've settled for the fact that you can take the boy out of the farm but… well. His heart is always going to be on the land, in nature. After all, who can compete with nature? It would be a formidable contest to even try to compare the wondrous works of the Creator of heaven and earth.

What I've found out is that if you're committed to any relationship there is usually a way to work things out. A brilliant explanation of this is a book by Stephen Covey. It's called "The Third Alternative". It's about both parties laying down a little of what they want so that together they can find another more creative way to come to agreement. This is the third alternative.

I'm getting ahead of myself but in our wedding bands we had a scripture engraved that in essence says, "God is the go between". The verse actually reads, "The Lord your God in the midst is mighty". It means the same and more. This has always proven to work for David and me. We are as different in our approach to life as any two people could be, but when we defer to asking God and asking each other what we think about any given situation that requires resolution, we find we can come to agreement eventually. Of course sometimes it takes time and effort, but when we do, when we try to listen then discover something we had never thought of, it always turns out to be the most beneficial and satisfactory way forward for both of us. To yield just something for the sake of unity in relationship is always a step to higher ground.

Another really useful attitude we have pretty much always maintained is to respect each other's uniqueness as two people. This we have found gives us both room to pursue our own goals. Remember that tree he saw? There is a richness in relationship when we see and foster another person's growth in any given area. We have done much together and much apart, while always supporting each other completely.

I've found that when I close off to a person because I am finding it painful to keep open to their sheer difference of opinions and actions, I automatically live in that space of what is known as apartheid or 'apart from'. It really makes an arrogant statement about who is right or wrong. In actual fact what is so valuable to relationship is often our basic human differences. With a generosity of spirit we can eventually find we learn things, while staying apart from that person can actually cost us the lack of insights that might be of great value to us in the long run.

I know because I've done this. For instance I've sometimes been so exhausted by 'needy' people (we are ordained pastors) – lots of years of people and listening over and over to everyone's nightmares – I've sometimes tended to withdraw in my own immaturity, even if briefly, when if I hadn't done so that person could have taught me patience and perseverance. It meant that in the end I had to go round the mountain to learn another way. We both lost.

Win/lose is a win for no one. In yielding and listening love wins. Love is win/win and involves an effort to achieve mutual understanding, which will in the end bring new insights that lead to compassion. It also makes it patently clear in Psalm 133 that the takeaway of unity is where God actually commands his blessing. And who doesn't want that? Courage to live in unity is one of our most valuable character traits. Courage to choose to yield, to be humble and to be kind, even to have faith at times.

The fact is when any relationship starts out there tends to be a dependence on one another, hardly ever wanting to be apart. If that continues too long it can swing the other way and eventually turn into independence. You know how a child starts out in total dependence, and then on into teen age where independence begins to surface. This can be good or it can be difficult, particularly if the teenager becomes so independent it seems like all advice appears to hamper their pursuits because they know better than any seasoned adult. While this is not always the case, if independence becomes fierce as can happen, it can lead to a breakdown in relationship that may take years to mend.

I have come to believe the ideal for marriage or any relationship to thrive and go forward is always going to be the way of interdependence. Dependence, independence and interdependence are all stages of relationship, but interdependence is the noble form of cooperation that best acknowledges the values in the other person. Non-communication is for the immature who seek only their own way. It embodies no virtues or graces, prevents reconciliation, and can manufacture such cruel and often undeserved rejection.

If a situation is talked through with civility, most things can be amicably resolved. Covey's great statement, "Seek first to understand and then to be understood", is of mega value as a life script. It allows both sides of the situation to be heard and respected. There's usually a way forward if we are prepared to act like grown ups. One thing is for sure, to give up our God given uniqueness is not the alternative that will grow good will. But to respect another's perspective and give them the grace of our acceptance of it is just plain civility.

I have found that both perseverance and determination are useful allies in most relationships. Kindness and the expression of it, not only in words but deeds, will usually make for a win/win in relationship. It's true, win/lose is always about control. The person who enforces a lose has a scarcity mentality that is fear based – the fear of losing control. Nothing in relationship works without grace and forgiveness. "Love makes allowances", 1 Corinthians chapter 13, and that's because we all need allowances.

I must tell you about the day David proposed to me. He had been sick and was living alone so my mother suggested he stay with us and she would ply him with her remedies to get rid of a flu bug he had for too long. I went off to work and when I arrived home at about five thirty, he called me into our living room where he was staying and sleeping on the sofa by a warm comforting fire. He was coughing and sniffling, he didn't seem to be a whole lot better for all of my mother's lemons and honey and whatever she so thoughtfully mixed up for him. She always had a heart to try to fix everything.

I walked into the room and he was there in his pyjamas and bathrobe. He never even said hello. He fell to one knee and said, "I've been thinking we should get married, will you marry me?" I was literally so shocked I couldn't even answer. He had to ask me three times before I finally said, "Yes, yes, I've been thinking that too and I'm sure, but I just didn't expect you to propose in your pyjamas!" He of course never commented on that except to say, "Don't come too close or you might catch this flu". "One enchanted evening" – thank you Rogers and Hammerstein – sounded great in "South Pacific" but...? A girl dreams of a proposal, and I'm sure I did, but I could never have dreamed that whole thing up. Then he said, "Go across the street to Jack's place," (Jack was a friend and a jeweller), "and choose a ring. Tell him I'll pay when I'm better". I mean...seriously...?

In one way we were perfectly content with what we were doing as a couple, singing together at all kinds of meetings and evangelistic crusades as they were called back then. However something triggered in both of us as we began to read over and over those verses from Isaiah: "Listen to me you islands, hear this you distant nations". It goes on to say, "He made my mouth like a sharpened sword, in the shadow of his hand he hid me". And then the kicker, "At just the right time – a light for the nations".

So much in that chapter told us – forewarned us – not to expect we would stay some sort of duo to entertain people or even evangelise people. We had only sung songs 'for the occasion'. It had never occurred to us that songs could be memorable enough that people would go home singing them, learning the truth of the words. The other thing that became obvious from somewhere deep in our hearts was that God wanted the people to sing to him, not just about him.

These things weren't in our thinking when we vowed we will wait, we will hide, we will become sharpened and we will do our best to hit the mark. The reaction to that and the cost of those next years was a price, like all of the prices since, that benefited more people than we could have possibly imagined. After a time of not being entirely satisfied with what we were doing, of feeling there had to be something more, we mutually decided we would stop everything we were involved with and wait until we did indeed feel like a sharp arrow that would hit the mark. Something more precise, more effective – this is what we sensed God was challenging us with.

We could never even begin to imagine the dilemma, the cost, the indignity we were about to experience as we went with great purpose and excitement to tell the heads of the groups we had been working with that we were taking time out. We told them this was because we wanted to be a whole lot more effective than we were, and how we longed to do something more significant than we had been doing. We also said we were sure it was God who had told us this and we quoted chapter and verse.

If it wasn't for the fact we were doing Christian ministry I would say, 'all hell broke loose'! It caused such a backlash. No one believed we were serious. Two of the three leaders we worked with accused us of being more interested in ourselves and the idea of our upcoming marriage than we were in 'serving the Lord'. I was stunned that anyone could think that about us but David, being his own man, never flinched at anyone's opinion if he was satisfied God had told him to do something. He just told me not to worry it would all work out.

All the insecurity and rejection I had inside me threw me into such dismay. It was my first taste of feeling sidelined by those of the same faith and it crushed me. David on the other hand moved right along, being totally assured things would be okay if we stuck to what we knew was the right thing to do. I felt like writing an Italian opera where I put the sharpened arrow through my heart. Yes, we are different.

In this uncomfortable period of time before we got married we found ourselves in no man's land and very misunderstood. We clung to the verse in Isaiah where it says: "At just the right time I will help you". For me it was so painful to turn down invitations to sing for things like our wonderful piano player Noel's big celebration for his twenty first birthday. He had supported us in everything we did and was always there to play for us. I begged David to say yes to him, just this once, but he stood firm, stronger in his faith and integrity than me, so we said no to Noel. It was a heartache and a price, a commitment we had made and there was no turning back.

There were many of those invitations, such a dilemma for me and such a no brainer for David. Did the man have a heart and soul? Well I knew he did, for God and for me, what more did I want? What we eventually had together was a life of wonder through being obedient to a God who never asks without repaying in full to overflowing with such love of a father who is so pleased by our faith in him that all the hard times in our lives can never outweigh the kind of party God puts on for us. To me that sunset was one of his best and most extravagant!

We were on the outer big time, misunderstood and talked about but once again it was Joy Dawson who had heard about what was going on. She came to us and told us she was going to 'ask God' for herself if we were really meant to give up all the things we had been doing. We never told her of our directive from the book of Isaiah and she never asked us any questions. She just wanted to know for herself. She loved us and truly cared if we were off on some crazy tangent.

She invited us to her home the following day. I was shaking in my shoes. David was so calm while all I wanted to do was scream, or run, or both. We arrived at the house, a home so many giants of the Christian faith had gone to over the years, a place where lives were changed forever. You knew whenever you went there it was no ordinary little house in Hillsborough. She was and still is, now in her ninth decade, a devoted and deeply spiritual person. Our Rachel inherited that same gene that runs through the Manins family. Black and white, no compromise, 'just deal with it'.

Joy always eyeballed you and never minced words so I knew there wasn't going to be a whole lot of small talk even though I was hoping for something, anything, to delay a tirade from another spiritual leader. She took one of my hands and one of David's and looked at us with such a love, I remember a glisten of tears in her eyes. She said in a very humble way that she was sorry we had been misunderstood and then she said, "God spoke to me from the book of Isaiah chapter 49 verse 23. I will read it to you both". I stood there thinking, I don't believe it, Isaiah 49. I was dumbfounded. I mean there are sixty six books in the bible with myriads of verses in them. That's some odds. To choose the book of Isaiah and chapter 49.

Here is what she read: "Those who wait for the Lord, will not be disappointed". Then in her decisive way she said very definitively that whatever it was God had told us to wait for, it would be something unbelievably good and not to let our faith waver because God would see to it that our waiting would not be in vain. I was nearly passing out with relief and total amazement at the whole thing that had seemed so shameful to everyone else.

That said she added, "Do you want to stay for a cup of tea, I've made date scones?" I had never experienced anything like it before. Curiously enough one of her names is Adeline. It was a huge lesson to me of the gracious loving nature of God, and like others who walked over her doorstep, I was never the same again.

We were married a few months later and went straight to Dunedin. I wondered from time to time if we would ever sing together again. Dunedin was like another country, another climate, another way of doing life. It assailed my sensibilities because there was nothing familiar to me. In my mind Dunedin was as remote as anywhere could be; a city with a hardy Scottish heritage, quaint and so extraordinarily cold to me coming from a subtropical climate. It seemed that in a moment of time all the fun, the friendships, the family, all I had ever known, were gone in a flash of a two hour plane ride.

Those years, three in all, turned out to be both my nemesis and my liberation. My enlightenment, my fighting chance and inevitably my power of choice, and as I trained myself to make right choices it became my emancipation. Pain can be for our own good, although I wished many times there was another way. 'Un mal pour un bien', in other words, some situations might seem awkward and difficult on the surface, but they could also turn out to be a blessing in disguise.

We got married in Auckland in a small chapel with an adjoining recording studio where we made all of our radio broadcasts. It was the end of one of those Indian summers that flowed its way into autumn with a beguiling reluctance. Still warm, such very beautiful clear days. I made the dresses for my bridesmaids, my own dress and my mother's as well. My grandmother made hers – black taffeta I bought for her at the classy department store called Milne and Choyce. I decided on a different bouquet of the deepest red roses and ambrosial lush red begonias.

I was, I suppose, always thinking of different creative ways to do things, which has served me well in my later life. I rented lots of palm trees and gigantic urns of luscious cream orchids for the front of the very plain Brethren chapel. It was tropical and I suppose rather avant garde for back then. I was working in a creative world of style and fashion, and I guess it rubbed off because I hauled in every prop I could to beautify the stark building.

My very proud father walked me down the aisle to a song David and I had prerecorded for the occasion. I walked towards David who was probably thinking, why am I standing in a veritable jungle? The song, a lovely old hymn in King James English, was a petition that matched totally with the sincerity of our hearts, for all we have ever wanted was to have the blessing of God on all we do. I have never forgotten the words, nor have I forgotten the tears I saw in people's eyes as the words fell softly over us all. The recording was playing and together we were singing from deep within our hearts:

> "Lord Jesus Christ we seek thy face
> Within the veil we bow the knee
> Now let thy glory fill this place
> And bless us while we wait on thee."

That little prayer we sang has been a catalyst in our marriage, the blessing of God in all its abundance has been ours throughout these nearly six decades together. All that has happened 'for better or worse' has never been devoid of God's love upon us like spring rain watering the earth. God is love, God is good all the time, I am utterly captivated by his love.

We had found a little cottage to rent in Dunedin while we were on our honeymoon. I suppose when in love one can be careless as only the young can be, heedless of how it works in that very innocent and euphoric state of mind. Oh I could fix up the cottage and yes we would survive with the two bar heater in the living room. I would cook those meals like Grandma and my mother always did. Things would be fine because in three years we would be back to the warmth, to our friends and family... it would fly by.

What I've found is that yes life does go on whether it tows us along, rolls right over us, or we learn to roll with it. I am obviously aware that our personal journeys and how we do life is tied to our own uniqueness. I'm also very aware that what I'm sharing with you is my own personal knowledge I've discovered over decades. I confess life has all but rolled over me on many occasions to where I had to find enough grit to just get up and carry on. I'm not assuming either that I'm here to instruct you to where I can give you the last word on anything. The shortcuts I give you are really just an accumulation of why I do what I do, how I got to where I am.

Within us all are such wondrous capabilities that have been carefully woven into our very beings from our conception. It's a continual discovery over a lifetime I suppose. If you had told me that first day in our little cottage as we tacitly walked around the freezing empty space, that I might one day cook a surprisingly good meal, or go on to cook meals for a hundred people, three hundred people (with help of course), while at the same time decorate a room, a birthday cake, a wedding cake or any of that stuff that is second nature to me now, I'm not sure how I would have reacted. A full on panic attack might have been a viable option.

I don't know how many times I have had read the epic Psalm 139 describing how intricately and wonderfully I have been made. By now you will be aware I believed parts of me worked well while the rest was like a dormant rock overgrown by all the wrong thoughts, comparisons and confessions of how 'I never had a brain in my head', yet eventually learned the brain I did have was the only one I needed. I am also aware of our fragility and how at times we can be living to our potential while at other times it's way beyond our reach.

What I have come to know is that when we are living as close as possible to our God given potential, a certain energy emerges from us that will never exist through any other person – past, present or future. A force, a masterpiece of creation never to be repeated in the same way ever again in another human. Like our DNA, there are no two blades of grass ever exactly the same. It's astounding how intricately we are made to be unique. The sound of your laughter, the depth of your curiosity, the strength of your tender touch, the healing of your acceptance, what is you, what is me. We are so quick to say, 'it's only me', and yes it is: the one and only me; the only one you.

Martin Luther King Jr, one of the greatest men to walk the earth, a peaceful activist calling for 'justice to roll down' for racial equality in America, was shot dead standing on the balcony of a motel by troubled racist James Earl Ray in 1968. Dr King said something so profound that it was one of the facets of truth that became a game changer for me. I quote him with all the respect in the world:

"Everyone has the power for greatness,
not for fame, but greatness,
because greatness is determined by service."

Grandma had never even heard of him when she lived it out in front of me. Hospitality and service is my true jewel box, my true satisfaction, my absolute mission. I can tell you that without the component of being hospitable, our lives and the opportunities gifted to us would never have happened. We have relentlessly and always seen it as our great pleasure and privilege to open our home, our fridge, our pantry, our bank account, our time, our energy, and our entire lives, to serve and care for others. Me always making too much food, like Jesus and the twelve baskets full left over, and David literally bathing everywhere we have lived in prayer and blessing so that whoever stepped over our door got more, more of everything for their bodies and souls.

The worldwide influence of our music, I have to say, is to a huge extent due to being hospitable, as those of influence came, ate and spread word of us and what we were doing. Some amazing people from all corners of the world distributed our songs. Peter Wallis in England, Keith Chua in Singapore, Jimmy Moore in America and Helge Schneemann in South Africa. They along with John and Rosaline Muys believed in us and Scripture in Song – the ministry – to the point that they sacrificed so much on our behalf to see that people got to know the power of God's word put to music. There were others in Europe including Youth With A Mission who spread our songs far and wide. They are all the kind of rare people who hear and obey what they are convinced God is telling them.

Standing in that little house I knew nothing much at all about service, my own uniqueness or that there was any ability in me to do things like serving a cause greater than myself. I now know this to be true though: the only way out of the prison of self is to serve another. It's what I saw those years ago as a child always feeling I had nothing to offer. Yet after some rather intense rearranging of my own life, it finally became my life long goal, and still is to this very day, to find a way to serve another.

That's for later because back standing in front of the tiny two bar heater and pondering my survival, though it might sound pathetic, I wish I had known some things about the awesome wonder of our humanity and the intricacy of us all — such fine detail has been placed within us. As the psalmist said:

> "Such knowledge is too wonderful for me,
> too great for me to understand.
> You made all the delicate inner parts of my body
> as you wove me together in my mother's womb.
> Thank you for making me so wonderfully complex
> your workmanship is marvellous.
> You saw me before I was born and
> every day of my life was recorded in your book,
> every moment was laid out before a single day had
> ever passed."

Here are the scientific findings on that! They are identical. In our bodies are five hundred muscles, two hundred bones, seven miles of nerve fibre, all synchronised or you would not be reading this and turning pages.

Your heart beats thirty six million beats a year and it pumps your blood through more than sixty thousand miles of veins and arteries, pumping more than six hundred thousand gallons each year. In all history here has never been such a machine created.

In time all steel and even the strongest metal will wear with use, but the layer God constructed around us – our skin – constantly renews itself, replacing old cells with new ones.

Our lungs are like portholes – filters that support us even in the vilest environments of our own making. They labour to sieve out wastes through six hundred million pockets of folded flesh.

Each second within our five quarts of blood, two million blood cells die to be replaced by two million more in a resurrection that has continued since we were born.

Thirteen billion nerve cells in our brain file every perception, sound, taste, smell, pain, touch. Within us is enough atomic energy to destroy a great city and rebuild it.

This research was provided by Og Mandino whose small books about God's miracles are really astounding. Yes God created us as awesome beings indeed.

As I stood there in my first home I was afraid and I stayed that way. Things kept falling in around me through what I perceived as an inability to cope with my ignorance, my procrastination and my sheer denial that this wasn't really happening. I was in no man's land. This little cottage with its faded elegance fuelled my excuses to the point where I surrendered what power I had to create a home. I had my eyes fixed on the obstacles both of my own making and of others who had never encouraged me to do better. I didn't know an obstacle was a moment of chance; a choice to take a step and move on. It was going to take me longer than it took the tortoise and his significant other to make it to the ark.

It's a fact that only you can do the things that make you the gift you are. If you have breath in your body, just a smile can go a long way to take care of an ache in someone's heart. It's taken me a long time to realise my own self worth, too long, but then again my face isn't a labyrinth of lines for nothing. The wonder for me is both my journey and how I was made to fit it so perfectly. I've found that the more we learn about how we have been created, the more perspective we garner and eventually we come to treasure just how miraculously we have been put together.

Then something happened that changed my life forever. It was so out of left field I never saw it coming. I just answered a knock on the door.

Rachel and Carol Guise, teacher/nanny.

Homework on the road.

The girls at the original KFC in Kentucky.

The girls in upstate New York.

The girls at Disneyland.

Linda McGowan and David in Switzerland.

Al Akimoff, with a pastor and family, in communist Poland.

Reona Peterson, Barbara Eccles (nanny/teacher), Paula Kirby, Don Stephens, Paul Hawkins.

The Garratts with Pianist Rod Wallace and teacher/nanny Marianne Duguid.

Patti and Rick Ridings Jay Ulrich, Rod Wallace at the Montreal Olympic Games.

Rod Wallace and Dale in Israel.

Dale and Joy Dawson in California.

David and Dale in Capetown, South Africa.

With Jamie and Jimmy Owens, Pat and Shirley Boone.

With Cliff Barrows and Daniebelle Hall, USA.

Landa Cope with Dale in Thailand.

Luke and Marieta Kaa-Morgan in Auckland.

Stephen Bell-Booth with Dale in Singapore.

Dale, Mindy, Ihaka with Kim and Paul Young in Auckland.

Roly and Claire Houghton in Auckland.

Wyn and Shirley Fountain in Auckland.

Jimmy and Carol Owens, Joy and Jim Dawson in Los Angeles.

With John and Joyce Hawkesby, Ray McVinnie in Melbourne.

Peter and Donna Jordan, Barbara and Bruce Thompson, Eliane Rees-Thomas in Hawaii.

Derek and Ruth Prince in Israel.

Dawn Goslin, Landa Cope, Fiona Gifford and Dale in Switzerland.

Kate Billington and Dale in Auckland.

Fae and Winkie Pratney, Dale and Rod in Texas.

Jeffrey Howie and Mindy in Texas.

Melody Green, Viv, Jamie Owens and Dale in California.

Mindy and Kate Hawkesby in Auckland.

Mindy and Jess Collins in Hollywood.

Mindy and Lynnda Owens, California.

Kona girls in Hawaii.

Bernadette and Phil Keaggy with Dale in Auckland.

Dan and Jamie Collins with Mindy in California.

Annette and Rex Horne with Dale in Sydney.

Shar Allen with Amelia and Ihaka in Auckland.

Mindy, Bradley and Susan Grose and Melody Green in California.

Dale, Dan and Jamie Collins, Carol Owens and Andrae Crouch in Texas.

Mindy and Bob Fitts in Honolulu.

Jess Collins and Dale, California.

Benny Prasad and David in India.

The Valle and Halvorsen families in Kona.

Dale, Stephanie Overton and Mindy in Auckland.

Dale and Graham Kerr Cooking at our home in Auckland.

Lynnda Owens and Dale in California.

Mindy and Buddy Owens in California.

Chapter 8

"Don't put it down
put it away..."
JAM

The Church Lady

She was as thin as a pin, neatly permed grey hair with a lavender hue, and groomed much like Queen Elizabeth II (only not so well endowed!). Out of the blue she came to see me, she had brought with her a brown paper bag of freshly made peanut brownies. A Kiwi icon in the baking stakes, these biscuits, as we call them, were what everyone in the entire nation (except me it seems) learned to make when they were twelve. At twelve Melinda was churning out enough apple muffins she could open a shop! At twelve I was dreaming, dancing and doing a bit of sewing on the side: it was all about me.

My visitor let her eyes roam casually around my living room and took in the spectacle of chaos and clutter that was my sorry attempt at housekeeping. By now I was a several months pregnant, nauseous, tired, lonely elephant. The smell of the brownies, warm and sugary, nearly sent me running towards the bathroom where I seemed to spend inordinate amounts of time anyway. Morning sickness must be a term invented by a male who never had it, as I see it, because for me the morning lasted all day and into night for each pregnancy.

By some miracle I managed to avoid having to excuse myself. I moved the pile of laundry to one end of the sofa so she could sit down. I was being scrutinised in the nicest of ways, she could see I was out of my depth, so overwhelmed and seriously incompetent. She wasn't unkind in any way, after all she was the only church lady who gave a nod to my existence. She cared enough to work out that I was young, missing my friends and family, and obviously had no skills in homemaking. That part screamed at her.

I swear as I looked at the piles of books, clothes, newspapers, fabrics, patterns of baby clothes all over the table, my sewing machine, laundry to be folded all over the sofa and chairs, it all grew before my eyes – small mountains of things never made for cohabitation. The embarrassment of it didn't register with me at that moment, though it would serve me well at some point later on. Humiliation can do that for you. Obviously it was one of those 'it's going to get worse before it gets better' situations. Why had I opened the door? Well in the deepest part of me I'm sure it was from sheer loneliness.

Overnight change? I don't think so, but here's the thing. When we are disgusted with ourselves it is often a reality check, a useful intervention for change. Because I'd managed to cover up my disorganisation by shoving it away on other occasions, I hadn't seen it as another person would. Now the other person was right there in amongst it. All of a sudden the truth of the utter mess I was in was painfully clear to me. I had no way out. I could never fix it because it had always been so perfectly fixed for me by my mother and grandmother. Where were they now when I needed them so badly? The truth of it was I had been a guest in their homes. I'd had staff of my own until we married and moved away. I didn't come to that realisation until after the church lady had gone, I don't even remember her telling me her name.

Right then all I was thinking was would she... could she... just go. After a twenty minute hour, she stood and said she would have to be leaving. She had to complete her housework, she said, and finish her dinner preparation. What in the world? It was eleven in the morning and I never even gave dinner or the preparation of it one thought at that time of day. Truth is I don't have to give it much thought these days either, but it's because I've learned how to do the prep and make a meal at record speed for the most part. In case you don't know, I'm going to tell you how. Oh and then she said, 'housework', I had missed the last bit that said 'work'. I just lived in the house. So you could prepare food, even an evening meal, in advance? That was an entirely new and novel concept to me. We were not in each other's orbit. Then there was the thing of completing housework. She had to be kidding. Only she wasn't.

As she was about to leave it was then I noticed my shoes covered in mud just lying there. I began to open the front door for her, my eyes on her and my feet manoeuvering the shoes aside. I used them to go to the mailbox. It was like the final insult. Of course my dad had always cleaned my shoes, he was nowhere handy either. I was in a rough and unforgiving sea where I had been cut adrift. No one to rescue me any more.

The relief when she made it to the doorstep was for me pure joy. I wanted her to leave more than I wanted a long happy life. She was leaving and I could feel the determination rise within me: I was never, ever going to answer the door again until I had shoved everything away first. I had just enough of Adeline's dignity running uncut through my veins to at least put on a show if I needed to!! Really my problem was I just needed a bit of warning so I could do a quick whip around, a bit of a tidy up, only she had arrived without any notice. I'd been busted. You might know the feeling. Now she was going to be gone what could possibly go wrong?

I have to tell you it was on that very doorstep at 1 Brent Street in Dunedin, on a miserably cold grey winter's day, that the sky might as well have fallen on my head. As I stood there, waves of nausea engulfing me, I had no notion whatsoever that nothing would ever be the same for me. It was like the heavens opened – angels sang hallelujah and I had been blessed with a clue, a way to do life that has been profound for me.

Her next wondrous words were the sound of my future and became a non-negotiable in my life. She tucked her brown leather purse neatly under her arm, patted me on the shoulder and amiably but resolutely, so I couldn't miss the point, looked at me with a twinkle in her eye. Letting out a small sigh she said, "My dear, I live by the saying 'don't put it DOWN, put it AWAY'." She would never know that with that little phrase, she had given me a gift, a gift of the freedom I would come to know over time. It would become one of my imperatives; a paramount practice and foundation to free me for my future acts of serving others.

When we married I had such ideals of how I would cook for people and care for them the way all of my family did. My ambition wasn't to be an expert and no sadly I'm still not. I didn't even have a notion of being so organised at homemaking that if I had the chance I'd straighten the Leaning Tower of Pisa. In a way I guess I just wanted to follow my family's example. The way I grew up. It was about the food, the generosity of it and the tantalising preparation and presentation of it that was so comforting to people. It was about a listening ear that was such a gift it had a way into people's hearts, it was the feel of abundance and the taste of satisfaction.

I understand now that what they did came from caring enough to make an effort because the love of giving was primary, no matter how few ingredients were at hand. Something for palate and heart always seemed to be created, both with food and ambience, to the point where you could genuinely taste what being loved was like. It's different from being told what it's like. Food without those ingredients – effort and love – is well – just food. Sometimes that can be enough, but going the second mile to care and comfort brings a finer result.

A man called Victor came to see my dad sometimes. He had a yellow tattoo on his wrist and a blue one on his leg, etched on him when he was packed off to a prison camp for Jewish people in Germany. There was a number on his wrist and another one, a Star of David, on his leg. He had no friends but my father Rudolph loved him. His own suffering gave him a certain kind of empathy that only comes when you know suffering yourself. I saw it in my beloved father, the kindest most caring of men.

Victor had escaped, come to New Zealand and through my dad had found human kindness did still exist. Dad had his own speciality – great thick hand cut fries and delicious fish from his sister – he made on Sunday evenings. I don't know if it was kosher but Victor ate with such gratitude, just to be at a table where he could recover some of his dignity – the return of his chutzpah, that amazing quality known to those of Hebrew heritage.

So I wanted to own that life for myself, to be there making food for people, because food is such a metaphor for love, even if you don't say so. It's a language I use when sometimes I don't know which words to use. When there's pain, grief, loneliness and loss, those times I often take a meal to someone or David takes it for me and stays and tries to listen and comfort. There are those times, so many of them! In fact this book would have been done years before if not for the doing of just that.

Unbeknown to me, my family showed me this life of hospitality, especially Grandma Adeline, and how without me even being cognisant of the thought, her inveterate self struggled and sought to work its way out of me. I'm sure back there at the beginning of my marriage she would never have believed what I would become.

I stood there on the doorstep as my church lady stepped through the gate and began disappearing down the little narrow street. She had such a way of owning her communication style, the same way another person owned their most comfortable shoes. Off she went. She never looked back, she never came back, I never did see her ever again. 'Don't put it down, put it away', the phrase rang in my ears. I just stood like a deer in the headlights, struck by seven words that would become a lifeline to me if I could just reach out and grab them, own them for myself.

All of a sudden I remembered how cold I had become standing there, so I quickly locked the door and went back to my living room. I began to think. I did have a system: when people were coming I'd move things. Maybe you're thinking I was decorating all the time? No, no, no, my decor was staring me right in the face. The 'look' had been effortless to create. It wasn't an 'on purpose' thing where you went out and bought collectables, the kind that with a little sandpaper and paint became shabby chic. Oh no, it was altogether different, much more unique, a style some might have preferred to think of as a disaster but I preferred to think of it as 'standard operating procedure'. 'Early junkyard' perhaps? Well at least until that day when I slammed headlong into the fact that denial is not just a river in Egypt, it is a state of mind. If you don't face up to something and own it you can never really change it.

Here was my problem, let's just say multiple problems on so many levels. What the church lady told me was the mother of all wake up calls. Now at this moment of this very day so many decades later, would you believe I too have come to live by the same saying. As I look back though, to even begin to practice anything vaguely like the idea of 'a place for everything and everything in its place' would involve me making choices that were going to require some very unfamiliar behaviours for me. Way out of my familiar comfort zone.

I looked around… it seemed as though everything had turned into triffids. Pile upon pile of things absolutely everywhere. I had this behaviour down perfectly though. If anyone was coming over all I had to do was open cupboards and shove. Run around the bedroom and collect the clothes off of the floor. We even had a built in closet I could use for such emergencies. David was a spreader so he had stuff in every room. All spread out ready for whatever it was he planned to do. Planned would have been the dubious word for his approach. I say no more. On the other hand I liked it a little more neat and tidy. So I put things in piles but those piles just went up and up and up!

That day I remember standing there in front of the two bar wall heater—we only had heat in one room. I was overcome with a shame so tangible it was like a kind of stranglehold. Procrastination, the 'silent assassin', my own well perfected procrastination, my well honed lazy approach to any kind of hard work, or any work for that matter, had dobbed me in, let me down in front of a very kind and thoughtful person who had made an effort to come to see me. I was mortified.

I could feel myself beginning to go to that fall back position I mentioned before. It's convenient, it's an idea, but it's not a good idea. It's blame shifting and it takes the heat off you. It's someone else's fault. Nothing in me had the common sense to know that my sloppiness, how I lived, was a career I had made for myself. It's how I truly was, what I had become with no one there to pick up after me, no one to take care of laundry, cook dinner and worst of all, no one to feel sorry for me. I must admit I was doing a pretty good job of that for myself as I stood there taking it all in.

David's mother told me she was pregnant for over twenty years. So right there you can imagine the environment was a 'no frills' situation. They just dealt in the 'Home Brand'. Having said that, his home was a marvellous 'one for all and all for one' huge happy family. Bible stories abounded and so did babies. It was like a finely tuned organisation that functioned perfectly. Industry was in place. Then there was me, all well turned out on the outside and all insecure on the inside. How I wished my new husband would see the no frills option wasn't actually working that well in my case. There we were, joined in holy matrimony, happy at the thought, but with not the slightest idea of how it worked.

I knew and so did he just what it was like to live in a home where you could pretty much always locate what you needed without sending out a search party. We both came from well run homes where the work ethic was 'de rigeur'. There were always flowers in the homes where I lived, not always special ones, sometimes even a bud vase with some sweet peas out of the garden. The bath was always clean. I had to put my head under the water to rinse my long hair as we never had a shower. The laundry was folded and put away the day it was dry, not a week later.

In Dunedin the two of us sometimes ran out of things to wear. It seemed like a permanent condition that David was destined to wear odd socks because, well, socks are demons determined to bring you down. They want you to buy more of them so they can be a majority around the place – or something like that. If it were only socks it would have been one thing, but it was becoming clear to me that I had painted myself into a corner. I could either carry on sewing clothes for the baby and ignoring the mess I was in. Or I could fall back into the blame thing that said I was never taught how – it was probably the war, school, those mean teachers and racist kids, the loss of my dream to be a dancer. Or I could admit I had thought of all that before because I felt unequal to the task of homemaking. Forgiveness clears so much of that up and helps you realise that for the most part everyone did their best; what they knew at the time.

I told you I was a train wreck but I bet you never really believed me. I want you to know these things about me and how I finally figured out what works for me. Maybe I can show you some short cuts. I know now we put ourselves through so many painful hoops to arrive at the fact that other people have drilled their way to the other side of that rock before us. So far I have attempted to lay out my life, my story and how I arrived at that day in Dunedin. I wish someone had pointed out to me how to take some shortcuts. I know we all have to live and learn but hey, sometimes even without consulting the instruction manual, we can get it to work by just looking at the pictures. You might be that kind of person though sadly this is hardly ever the case.

My future life was to be a process of learning from others, and always trying to stay informed by reading constantly and widely as I have done for many years. I am forever asking questions of people I trust who are wiser than I am. There's an abundance of them! As I have grown old I've come to understand some things about life that only a long journey can gift us with, so now when certain things happen I find it easier to cope, at least in some ways, with a lifetime of experience behind me. There is so much more I can access to help and sustain me. Now when taking an unknown path, somehow there are certain familiar guideposts because of all that has been accumulated in the process of my life.

It's very different when we are young, because at that stage we don't have the weaponry to combat our painful experiences in the same way. There's not so much we can use as a reference to help us. It's simply not possible for the young to have 'old knowledge'. Over time our principles and character are formed by our choices. Sometimes for the young it is especially overwhelming to bear things alone. I understand that. I often felt alone, even with all the people around me, because they were too preoccupied with their own survival. It's clear to me now. All that was required of me was to look pretty and have a happy face even when I was confused, but I always felt God comforting me.

I feel privileged to have learned so many things and to have had the opportunity and knowledge available for me to retrain myself. In a way I have discovered a whole new DNA in what I think and what I do, and in many ways that has served me better. I can't tell you things like how I saved for my retirement, for one thing I have never retired, I just keep going. How I wish I'd even known about things like meditation, which I've taught myself as a lifesaver for the storms. And mindfulness – just being grateful for now, just to be here now, just to appreciate now, is to me one of those ultimate gifts of living our best possible life, letting it flow and accepting it rather than fighting it.

When the mind tells the brain what we want to do or think, that outrageously cool brain of ours goes ahead and arranges it for us. We are not our mind; our mind will do what we tell it to do. To think and speak as we choose. I know I'm repeating myself and it may be just for myself. No one has the power to hijack my state of mind I just thought they did. Sometimes it's best to just close up that book full of disappointment and failures and, as Adeline did and for the sake of others, put the book away and compartmentalise… shut away the things that can't be solved, accept what we cannot change and leave the rest to God.

I had to realise – and its taken a while – that my mind and my emotions belong to only me and when I began to take ownership of them I could have a new beginning which brought a whole other outcome. I began, I guess you could say, to build my own internal reservoir where my real authenticity had a chance to emerge. I was becoming the me who wanted with all my heart to care. The more nobility and self acceptance came slowly and simply as I started making promises to myself and keeping them, it meant the less I needed others to fill up that reservoir. I began to understand that as Saint Francis said: "For it is in giving that we receive". I know for certain the only thing as valuable as my life is my honour.

It's freaky but all of these neuroscientists and the bible itself tell us: "As a person thinks in their heart, that is what that person becomes". Our brain has such plasticity it can continually change itself. It's wondrous to understand we don't have to think about what causes us pain unless we make a choice to, and then so many parts of our body respond in such a negative way. Conversely when we think and speak positively and gratefully we open the doors to endless possibilities.

We are after all created in the image of a Triune God, the master creator, redeemer and helper. Eventually I came to find out that we are in fact a masterpiece.

Chapter

9

daily leaf

earlier

the kitchen ~~first~~ (8

Omahu Road

My Extreme Makeover

As I went back inside my house it began to dawn on me that while I was mortified about being busted, it had to be true. There was a method to everything Adeline had done and I'd never begun to realise both the simplicity and at the same time the sheer industry of it. Simplicity because once I started on several major behaviours the rest seemed to fall into place.

With my heart and soul I have a deep desire that if you are unfamiliar with what I am about to tell you, then it's possible you may be where I was back then, but I promise you we can make a run for it together and you will love the outcome. If on the other hand routine and organisation is just what you do in your life, or if you have someone to do the time consuming stuff for you, you may find the next pages quite amusing anyway... or unbelievable.

In the space of about twenty minutes I had been given a chance, a way and then a how to get me going. As I stood there in the gloom of that winter's day, I had no idea in my wildest dreams that eventually so many thousands of blessings would weave together my own life of hospitality. It was always going to be about hospitality and that meant I needed to know the true essence of what that could be, with all its outcomes, complexities and privileges.

It was the reality of the end that I had in mind, even if I had no idea how to get from chaos to competence. I was to learn how to have the endurance necessary for the call that comes with the territory of caring for others. Hospitality can easily be mistaken for entertaining, and while that is a valid component of the art, if that's all it is, so many opportunities to enhance another's life can be lost. Opportunities we might never experience the privilege of having again.

It was April in New Zealand. We were in autumn heading to winter in every way. Some of our seasonal sojourns turn out to be more manageable and temperate, others can be rugged and harsh. Then again some passages of our lives are so beautiful, peaceful and sublime, our very souls seem warmer and we never want anything to change. Yet there is a time for everything. I wish it were not so sometimes though... for I find as far as timing goes in my own life, grief capriciously chooses whatever time it pleases. It haphazardly comes and goes, spreading its nostalgia, its stab of pain and then seems to depart like the mist. Those times are when I know the power and gravity of the strong arms of grace.

Well we progressed into a winter far too approximate to the Antarctic for me, and whether I gave recognition to the seasons of life or not, I really found myself in two winters at the same time. One was just the natural process of what the planet is made to do. It cools, it chills, it rests, and in that time it prepares to bring a new season. I would never have imagined my own interior winter of the next three years was preparing to bring forth something so rewarding that to this day I'm forever grateful. Yet although timing is everything, back at that time, like in all those times, you don't necessarily want to hear it when it seems like your timing is off. But it turns out the world is round and although that season seemed like the end, it would eventually become the beginning.

Auckland where I had always lived was so much warmer; I'd never been cold before, not like this. I didn't know loneliness and

I had never felt the unfamiliarity that began to gradually reach into my soul. I had no concept that to be challenged was a gift in different wrapping paper. All I knew was the terrain was totally unfamiliar to me; in fact everything that had been vaguely familiar had gone, vanished, almost as if it never existed. I was like that tree I've read about that survived a hundred years of avalanches and lightning strikes but was ironically brought down by a horde of small beetles.

I was certainly brought down and landed with a bump that was a whole new reality. Instead of a mother bringing me breakfast in bed (it was her way to say she loved me and although I protested constantly she still insisted), I now had a husband rushing out the door to work. Sometimes his hastily ironed shirt was even a bit damp. I didn't have the faintest knowledge of the life I would live over time, or even that I could somehow get out of my own road to give enough credence to the fact that there might be others I could care for. I would have had no way to believe such a thing was ever possible. But eventually I was able to step up, do the job I'd longed to do. Of course this would take time and the giving of my heart to the purpose.

It's as well I've always loved the prayer of St Francis which means my purpose was clear, "Let me not look for help so much as to help". However there is always a 'however' isn't there? Mine was that I had stuff to work on no one could fix but me. I'm living proof that one's story line can be changed. I thought about my life's experiences that seemed to have stolen most of my capabilities from me. That's how I perceived it. Yet perception is not fact, never will be, that's why we need to hear real stories and live in reality. Justice always hears two sides of a story. How else can one know 'is it really true?'.

Because I know better now, I've learned to challenge myself to fix my own attitude. If I had known then I would have reversed my thinking as an ingrate. I could have been thankful for all of the good things, the amazing things I did have. I never even remembered, as Adeline had taught me, to count my blessings and name them one by one. The gratitude list and the blame list are diametrically opposed behaviours: both can be learned but it's always up to us. If I'd thought about it I could have been thankful David had a good job, I could go to a beautiful city park and walk through such lovely gardens. I could have even been grateful that we had food on the table, which at a stretch resembled some kind of edible substance. That would have been the short list.

True gratitude knows no end and takes us on the incredible journey of believing there will be more and each day our daily bread will appear. Here's a quote from renowned life coach and therapist, Martha Beck:

> "Gratitude is the emotional sweet spot from which we can create our best lives. It takes us out of feeling like victims. The longer we stay in gratitude the more abundance we see, the more gratitude grows. When Jesus said, 'I come to give you life more abundant', I don't think he just meant padding our bank accounts, I think he meant filling every moment of our lives with more joy, fascination and passion. Research shows that mere stuff can't give us that kind of abundance. It comes from pushing our limits, from helping others, and especially from expressing gratitude."

Over time we become aware we all have a place that works for us when it comes to fixing ourselves. As much as we watch other people who seem to get it faster and better, we can only do what we can do. First it is essential we take enough time to set our own pace if we want to begin the fixing. Secondly, for me anyway, I had to learn how to monitor that pace so I would have an assurance I wasn't standing still, wishing for another easier way out of my own need out of a season. I had to learn that when I yielded to the good of it and embraced the grace for it, I would discover it would produce its own unique fruit.

I suppose I was struggling with the dialogue, 'it's just the way I am, it's the way I've always been'. It was obvious that to move forward at all, even at the pace I was going, I would have to cut off the rear view mirror. Fortunately by now I had come to terms with the fact that procrastination was truly the thief of time, and laziness was just as big a thief. I was beginning to have a 'change of mind' – that's the dictionary definition of the word 'repentance'. It's a good word; it's anything but negative, it's entirely positive if you give yourself to it.

Before I go on with my story I'm going to lay out for you what I've come to know as the essential components of what it meant to make the changes that eventually would become the new me. You'll find the story weaves in and out. One step forward, one step back, until eventually it all began to work. Although it took me a while to work it out, over time I found there were some essential elements within the process of change that meant it finally became possible. It's still my paradigm to this very day and I'm hoping it could be useful for you. So here's how I found this process worked for me:

- To always begin with the end in mind because what I aspired to was of the utmost importance to enable me to see further down the road to where I began to remove the obstacles and then reach the end in a way that eventually became second nature to me.

- To muster courage laced with a lot of grace and reading avidly about courageous people enabled me to work on self defeating behaviours. I realised people in far worse situations than mine had something in common – they never gave up.
- To make a list that would get me there, help me know where I was going and how to achieve the steps toward my goal.
- To set a time frame so I could complete the tasks.
- To make considered choices. The reward these brought meant I began to live in an orderly fashion that gifted me with the beauty of my surroundings. I still love that.
- To do the clean up. This automatically moved into the area of cooking as I taught myself to clean up as I went. The thought of a big cleanup at the end encouraged me to do things in a methodical way, like keeping the surfaces free, wiping down, and putting things away after I used them.
- To pace myself. I had to measure my strength because I was sick. Our energy levels depend on so many factors.
- To be prepared. Preparation for me became and still is everything. It means I have always been able to be present with the invited and uninvited. I have made a point of having my pantry and freezer stocked with basics so I'm never caught out. I've learned to buy two or more of what's on sale to take away the concern of wanting to make something but not having the right ingredients. I found it essential to keep a list so things could be replaced when they were beginning to run low.
- To have a faithful repertoire. I began to gather a repertoire of meals and learned never to try anything new on guests because

a surprise isn't always positive.

- To know hospitality and all the phases it takes to provide adequately. I know for sure that being personally part of the provision will always be where the pleasure is for both me and those at my table.

I wanted to give you these few tips as a guideline to the way it's worked for me over the years. It was imperative to capture the attitude of being open enough to change even though I had to wrestle it down. The wondrous thing is we can choose to change an attitude even though we can't change the past. For me both willingly and grudgingly to choose the right attitude meant I could actually change my future.

My past was only my past. I have found it helpful to revisit the good things because that put courage in me. The only reason to revisit the negative parts has been to seek any wisdom I could learn and just let the rest go. If I didn't do that, if I still don't do that now, I can get frozen to the spot of my failures and fears, and it's harder to forgive myself or anyone else.

After the church lady left, it didn't take too many days of pondering and ruminating on my situation before I realised I had come to a bend in the road. It didn't mean it was the end of the road unless I failed to take the turn – just because some things in me needed fixing, it didn't mean everything was broken. I realised that if my heart was made of marshmallow, my actions would be no better.

I began to find I had a willing heart, a heart that wanted and needed the journey of change. Falteringly I became aware I had to capture the backbone and whatever courage I could muster to contemplate a new lifestyle. I've tried to make sure I know where I want to go, what I want to achieve, and step by step head in that direction. Of course we all take a step backwards every once in a while. That's when we reach down deep for our well earned courage and grab it because it's there, no matter which school teacher said we were dumb, no matter who said we'd never make it.

We learn from history, and by observation which teaches and enriches us. I'm reconciled to the fact that things don't and can't always happen overnight, but in time if we keep making positive choices (and for me faith in God) we end up on the high road. It's not that it isn't just as bumpy up there, but grace has a way of smoothing things out. The low road is so over crowded anyway. We forget it took Edison over ten thousand failures before he invented the electric light bulb. His response after a failure is the classic: "That's not a mistake, it's an education".

Before I tell you what I did and how things bit by bit began falling into place, I want to show you from my own understanding what real courage and perseverance look like. It was imperative for me to truly have an end goal in mind. These two stories are both true and factual. There is no possible way my story would ever begin to match them in any conceivable way, but they are stories of courage and courage will always be the way forward, no matter what decisions we are faced with. Of course very few people will ever aspire to the fortitude of these heroes, but it's so inspirational to know the reality of their ethos, principles and sheer unrelenting dedication to their seemingly impossible goals.

Nelson Mandela was in Robben Island prison for twenty seven years. He, just like Viktor Frankl of Auschwitz, always had a goal, a destiny, a way to make the very best out of the very worst. The worst humans can do to other humans. Viktor Frankl and Nelson Mandela both believed in a time they would be free and would use their experiences of injustice as a means of freedom for others, for the betterment and advancement of violated humanity.

In almost three decades of unimaginable horror, the prison at Robben Island had to build an extra concrete wall around Mandela's cell because snipers were forever trying to kill him once night fell. He was allowed one visitor, once a year, for thirty minutes. If you go to his little house in Soweto, the tour guide will show you a room with a table on which stands a pair of ordinary black shoes. What is extraordinary about those shoes is the way the soles are worn down. An American forensic scientist who asked permission to take them away for analysis found whoever wore them had constantly run on the spot, probably for several hours at a time. Mandela's goal to stay fit was he would eventually be the man to lead his country out of apartheid... and he did.

Victor Frankl could have blamed the entire Third Reich from Hitler down but he made an amazing choice. He chose his own attitude. After being freed he went on to establish schools of Logo Therapy – finding the meaning of one's destiny and how to get there. The aim of the therapy was to lead people mentally and emotionally to become free of the experiences that had damaged their lives. His schools and teachings are based on believing anyone can be the best they can be.

He encouraged others, even the most desecrated people, to find what he called 'the spark of life' (you could say destiny), and to believe with them that they could achieve their goal from that little spark. This came out of doing all he could in the three appalling death camps where he was imprisoned as a Jew in Nazi Germany. It takes your breath away to imagine such perseverance, such altruistic and selfless forgiveness that brings healing not only to people but to nations. It is a true picture of what human courage at its best can look like.

I'm always amazed at a similar and valiant choice Mother Teresa made as she worked with the sick and dying on the streets of Calcutta. Her choice out of her most noble heart was always fraught with the ambiguity that she, in her own words, was never absolutely certain God loved her. She also suffered from depression but it never stopped her from spending her life in service of others. I've found it pays to know about people like these, for one thing it diminishes our own self pity for the circumstances we find ourselves in. A necessary reality check.

Well I could see just far enough around the bend to know one very vital thing: if I was ever going to change I would never do it without a goal first of all and then a plan. For me it had to be a day to day plan. Planning is a funny thing. The thought of a plan excites some people madly; they can't wait to lay it all out. At the same time the thought of planning can send other people into deep pondering like, 'I can't even get out of the chair to make a list for the proposed plan'. Well neither could I. How did it never occur to me that there's always a strategy where achievement is concerned. Ask any army general, 'let's just wait and see'. I don't think so. It's tactical.

So when I did get out of the chair and began to strategise, to my dismay I had to face up to the fact I couldn't believe how hard it was to get myself going. Then I had those niggling grudges. I absolutely had to let go of all that blame and all of those recriminations of 'I should' or 'I shouldn't have' or 'they should' or 'they shouldn't have'. Somewhere lurking in the back of my mind there might have been the ignoble thought, what if she comes back and I haven't done a thing?

To start with it was imperative for me to make a daily list – a list that would somehow help me with the phrase 'don't put it down put it away'. I had no one to hold me to it but it was my only option. The funny thing is I still make lists to this day and rarely do any kind of event, even a small dinner for more than our family, without a list. I made up other sayings like: 'see it and do it'; 'does this live in this room?' 'Will my clothes benefit from lying in a heap on the bedroom floor?' You couldn't possibly believe how difficult it was for me to action my plan. Old habits die hard, that's true.

I had to do another thing as well because in the beginning I kept thinking to myself, I've got all day, I'll easily get everything done… Are you kidding? So the next thing I had to do to make it work, can you believe, was to put time limits on myself. I was completely unfamiliar with self disciplines in these areas. Of course I did other things automatically, like taking a shower, but running a household – well no – not me – not ever before.

Everyone's capabilities are different and it can be more stressful than living in a mess if you push yourself too far too fast. Getting a routine together for myself meant keeping my tempo slow and steady until I knew I had begun to establish it. I guess I was retraining myself about fundamentals, the things I absolutely had to do each day. Simple disciplines, doing what I knew I should do, the things I knew would benefit both David and me and doing them without excuse. If for instance you want to take a vitamin C tablet every day to boost your immune system, you can't just take seven on Friday night because you never took one every day.

I began to find I could accomplish things on my list and as I crossed them off it felt so good. My capabilities slowly began to increase and so did my list because I hung up, put away and cleaned up. It only happened through dogged determination. It's a fact: success grows success. My 'coup de foudre' (that huge thunder clap) from the church lady was really my starting place to hold me to disciplines I had never learned or even contemplated. My list – a piece of paper – graduated to a daybook. Of course saying it into my phone is an option now but I like pen and paper, it's always been the same when I want to get something done.

Satisfaction is a huge motivator and as a paid up member of the sloth community, I need motivation to become satisfied. After all these years I guess I'm finally an alumni sloth member. The other great thing for me regarding the list was it acted like a stock take of my daily activities. It was helping me monitor my progress, maybe like the occasional weight check; it helps you stay on course. I was pleased when I could cross things off and sometimes I was disappointed I hadn't accomplished everything, but even then I found it seemed to make me want to do it better, do it right.

Whatever I just couldn't get done in one day (and that's not so unusual), I moved over to the next day. The thing I came to love and still do is the private victory that spoke to me of what I did when no one was looking. That meant I did it out of real integrity, which built a new and satisfying nobility in me. I was building my new self list by list. I was taking care of business; the business of making a home, of somewhere in the future becoming my best self. Well yes, I'm still working on that, but anything would have been an improvement.

If you don't have a home, chances are you have a room or part of a home. Whatever our area is where we live, it tells people how we do life, how we operate, what we love to have around us, and it also speaks of our personal disciplines. Right here I mean it when I say if I can put it away instead of down, I promise you anyone can.

You may be interested to know how I decided to clean up the kitchen. The kitchen and I were not at all familiar with each other, barely on speaking terms. There was a huge accumulation of things on the counter top that were homeless, just staring me down. This tiny kitchen did have a pantry of sorts so, with a fleeting scrap of motivation, one day I decided to put away everything that had always been left lying around. It was a lot of stuff. This is what I did.

There was no rhyme or reason to how I stacked my pantry, I just decided everything should be out of sight. It had never occurred to me the tall things should probably go at the back, graduating in sizes down to the front. The things that would expire first should be handy and the things that had expired shouldn't be there at all. I just picked it all up and shoved it on the shelves. Everything homeless had now gone back home, in no particular order, to where I could see what was there, to where I could see anything really, it was just all crammed in. There you go... whew! I was beginning to get the look of a kitchen that reminded me of Grandma because she never had anything around except those things she was working with at the time. A place for everything and everything in its place? I don't think so, not in this pantry.

I decided to look at magazines for something simple to cook. Most of the recipes in those days were easy and for people either on a low budget or for others like me who hadn't cooked very much. The fact is we were getting tired of toad in the hole. What is that you ask? It's English pork sausages baked in batter made with white refined flour, eggs, milk, fat and salt. Yikes, to think we survived that! Sometimes we ate mince (ground beef). I stirred frozen vegetables into it until eventually David planted us a fantastic vegetable garden. I'd never baked in my life and it's still not my favourite occupation, because I prefer to tamper with recipes and throw in ingredients as I taste rather than measure. I find baking has a precision to it that doesn't suit my personality disorder (make that disorders).

So now I was faced with two enormous problems. First I couldn't find anything in the pantry. It was a 'no fly zone'; you couldn't get in there, the homeless were jammed in so tight. Secondly I wanted to try out some new recipes but I'd never heard of cleaning up as you go, so there was the dismaying fact for me of the kitchen sink and its surrounds. Stuff was piling up and up and I was constantly running out of utensils and bowls. I think this was where I was about to start to persevere because I found I really loved cooking.

Unfortunately I was to discover the principle of how to stack a pantry applies to the fridge as well. It took me so much time to find anything that I spent almost more time looking than cooking. Such basic things so unknown to me, and if they are to you just try to follow my excessive, put it away in the right place, behaviour. You will come out somewhere in the middle, but at least not searching so long for a little jar of something squeezed in behind all those tall bottles… It's like being behind in the game and having to play twice as hard to win.

Although I wasn't cognisant of the fact, the truth was (and still is) that every moment of the journey would be necessary and it would have to be borne with patience and perseverance. I didn't know then, but I do now, that it's far more useful to begin, as I said before, with the end in mind, mainly because, there will always be an outcome no matter how hard or how long we have to endure to get there.

This applies to all self management issues because our past can hold us back from reaching our true potential and the goals we dream of in any area of our lives.

So although I'm discussing what I would call a very pedestrian issue that was simply how to free myself of the procrastination preventing me from getting going, it's the same for everyone who wants to take a bold step in their lives and accomplish more of their destiny. You have to start somewhere. Adeline's way of being ready and available – that mercurial mystery that eventually became my long and satisfying life of hospitality – was my goal. I had made my choice, falteringly but with all the courage I could lay my hands on at the time. I wish I had known self inquiry doesn't need to be self inflicted punishment for how we find ourselves to be, but rather a useful and effective way to change something that's going to be beneficial in the end.

I had to choose to let go of self pity and grow up. I couldn't contemplate a feverish pace because for one thing you will remember I was pregnant and unable to keep anything down. It was kind of funny because the day we called the doctor he never examined me, he just stood at the end of the bed and said, "What's all the fuss about, you should have come to see me. You didn't need a house visit, you're not sick, you're pregnant". I guess he missed the bedside manner part of his training as a GP.

When he told me I was going to have a baby I recall the panic, the uneasy thought of being alone, no family, no friends and David leaving for three months. He was to go on a trip that would take him to India, Sri Lanka and parts of Africa where there were vast tea and coffee plantations with their operating plants. He would learn and experience the entire business of how, with due process, to make an excellent cup of tea. In case you're wondering I don't make his tea for him, it's scary. For David it was an opportunity a twenty five year old would grasp and run with. For me it was a nightmare. All I wanted was to go with him, but it made no sense because of my pregnancy.

They say every problem you encounter is no more than a pebble in your shoe. When you walk a while with discomfort at first you hobble, sometimes you try to wriggle the pebble into a more comfortable spot, but very often when the shoe is removed it was really only a grain of sand. There were times I was still telling myself I'd get round to organising things. The lies we tell ourselves are all part of our perfunctory nature that means the more we get over ourselves and our excuses, the more we defeat our ego. By ego I mean the part of us that comes from being self centred.

My plan had to be simple otherwise I knew I would disappoint myself and become so discouraged it would lead me back to lethargy again, but to not move on wasn't an option because atrophy had lost its appeal. The interesting thing is the goal, the plan, the list, meant the obstacles were really only irritants that kept me from seeing properly when I took my eyes off my goal. Those obstacles I've encountered have always been quite uncompromising, and I've found them to be useful because they have acted like agents of change to spur me on.

I am aware that so much has changed since I stood in that little house in Dunedin back then. I thought I'd marry David, live happily ever after and it would be a bed of roses. The fact is that David was not my problem; he's always been my encourager. Some of the changes that have happened over my almost eight decades are huge ones we all know. Those like cyber technology, automation of every kind, scientific advancement, to name a mere few. Then there's the amusing stuff like the fact that men wore hats until President Kennedy went hatless to his inauguration. That was pretty much the end of that. I remember when Sean Connery took off his tie and wore a turtleneck sweater. 'How amazing', people said. I have to say he couldn't look bad in anything!

Yep, it's all different, although every generation is the same: change is always a certainty. Yet human nature hasn't changed, it turns out we all have the same struggles as the generation before. The need for courage, honesty, perseverance, tolerance and an open heart are always going to be the way forward on so many issues we face. At the same time, standing like a rock on our principles will always make our lives transparent and true. The absolutes of our life must remain absolute; what we will and will not do. Oscar Wilde said regarding authenticity, "Ordinary riches can be stolen, real riches cannot". Some of our greatest riches in the end are our principles and what they are based on.

As well in our souls there are infinitely precious things that cannot be taken from us. I have a poet's heart though I don't write poetry, but things materialise in front of me that make me gasp so often. I love the wonder of God's creation; I have hardly ever missed gazing at a full moon. It's a thing my granddaughter Millie and I share, we still have that precious heart connection when we see it. Sometimes we just text one another: "Full moon". It seems a shame to take something so breathtaking for granted. Acorns – they feed them to pigs – and yet in the spring a mighty oak puts on a display of peridot green as wondrous as the precious stone itself. The acorn, just like us, holds within it the wondrous unfolding of what can look like an impossible outcome.

For sure the idea of goals was becoming more of a reality. Because of that knowing/doing gap, it seemed the end was still 'somewhere over the rainbow', but I was heading there no matter how long it took me. Grit and grace are good partners. Of course your goals and mine can't possibly be alike; the choice of where you're headed is entirely yours. So I carefully advise that if you're anything like I was, you might like to consider your own routine. Just sit down and work out your plan to succeed realistically.

I found once things I wanted to achieve were written down, I began to move forward toward reaching my goals with so much more intent. Doing one thing at a time was good because it was developing the art of concentration to complete the task. Neuroscientists are not for multi tasking interestingly enough.

Ghandi said, "Our greatness is not so much being able to remake the world, but being able to remake ourselves". My list looked a bit like an army requisition, but eventually I found every exit was an entry to a somewhere else. I had some splendid failures on the way as I endeavoured to clear my mind of 'I can't'. I also felt if I took a good look at how I did something successfully it proved helpful for me the next time. To examine our behaviours is a worthwhile thing to do. Like going to the grocery store then actually putting everything away when I got home right then and there! Oh yeah, that was a big deal for me, 'see it and do it'.

Everything seems to have its own reward; inertia had reaped its own reward with me and so did having a routine. The way I am, how I have developed as a homemaker, is more about getting the job done and doing it properly before I kick back. This is something I impose only on myself. You need to do what works for you. It's all about the stage of life you're at, but if we don't seize the day, something or someone else will – it's gone – just like that...

They say it takes three weeks to three months to really change a habit so the new one becomes a life style. It's important to remember too that failure is a short lived event, not a person, not ourselves. Making small intentional choices in everything meant my capabilities slowly began to increase.

Choose a habit – it's always going to be a choice. Exercise, the way we eat, what we eat, how much for instance. I'll give you an example to help you understand what I mean. My brother once said to me, "I always stop eating before I feel too full". I found that advice invaluable because I often went away from the table feeling too full. Making that a habit as far as food is concerned is something I have found very beneficial. It's all just turning a decision into a routine. I put away, I cleaned up and instead of just crashing over the finish line each day even though all my tasks weren't necessarily done, I felt satisfied I'd at least made an effort and of course grace runs to meet us as we reach for change.

There's an upside to having a list staring you down though, it removes that menacing thought of 'how will I remember all those things?'. It might be a phone call or text to a lonely, sick or grieving person. It could put courage in them just knowing someone cares. It's also easy to arrange things in order of priorities which are the longer, bigger jobs, usually the ones you don't really want to do. How to flash through the smaller easier ones like making the bed. I had to put that first because as I was sick right through both pregnancies, if I didn't get up and make the bed I'd get right back into it.

Somehow I'd hitched my wagon to the church lady. It was as though she had been sent to give me a way that would inspire me to take my first step towards my future. However the choice was entirely mine. If I had let the opportunity pass, like with all opportunities, there would be no way of knowing how the future would turn out. I started experimenting with the easiest and fastest ways to do things. It's just a way to build creative self management and self control – well that can't hurt! It spills over into all sorts of areas – like the portion control where food is concerned. Now I have shrunk four inches (it's a trick old people do). I'm thankful I have enough discipline in me to really control my portions because I can't go up anymore, only out, and that can't be good.

As I went from room to room I taught myself to always try to take with me the things that don't belong in that particular space. 'Wait a minute', you say, 'I have four kids, a dog and three cats'. Yes, I understand, and that means you clean up at the end of the day or you'd always be picking up. That's why our plan and our list must suit us individually. Who said kids can't put away? Start them young; it will build their character.

Some people work best earlier in the day, others are night people. Of course the optimum for me now is to just get on with it, but to tell the truth I can hardly speak English until I've had coffee in the morning and I never go to sleep before eleven thirty or midnight. So a morning person I am not, I just do things like a robot at first.

We all have a different work ethic and just like diets or supplements for health, you can never generalise. What suits one doesn't suit another. There are so many things to be factored in. I just happen to be high octane by nine or ten in the morning and I'm off like a rocket driving everyone crazy. Getting dinner prep organised, list for the store, whatever is important for that day, and if something big is coming up there will be prep for that as well. I like to get as much done as I can at my highest energy level. I guess the sloth in me just gave up and slunk away, but as I said, drilling through the rock of inertia was no easy task and it sure took a while.

I prefer to think of personal disciplines as a dance; a dance of satisfaction and freedom. After a while I began thinking of what I 'could do', not what 'I couldn't do'! Whatever we think turns into an action, actions deliver consequences, and for me it will always be about habits and how I choose to develop them to serve or frustrate me. I don't want to keep saying I'll do it later, because it doesn't feel as good to me as just getting on with it. It's a smart thing to do the stuff we hate when no one else is looking, like taking an extra minute to take the fluff out of the dryer or to empty the vacuum cleaner for the next person who uses it. What we do and how we do it by ourselves is our real selves.

Here's another marvellous thing for me. I was beginning to know exactly where everything was and that took a lot of stress and frustration off me. Instead of wasting all that time looking for something, I was finding 'a place for everything and everything in its place'. Of course I'm forever working on behaviours, those habits I wish I didn't have. We are all just that work in progress. But to get things done in order to have time to do things for others was always something I aspired to and truthfully it's the same to this very day. A person wrapped up in themselves makes a pretty small parcel.

One thing I'm still learning is that art of just stopping every so often. In the end I've found I do a better job if I take some time to relax here and there. Because I'm energetic I find it very hard to stop once I get going. If I see things that need doing I still tend to run at them, but I know I do better when I refresh better. Are athletes the only people who know if there is energy expenditure there needs to be equivalent recovery time? I think I'm finally getting it, but to apologise and say 'no' because I simply can't fit it in rather than be a martyr at my own expense, for me is the hardest thing ever.

I wish I was one of those people who could just lie down and let it all go on around me, but instead I'm the type who finds myself lying down and standing up on the inside. David on the other hand will lie down and relax for about twenty minutes anytime. It works for him, but then I probably would do it too if I got up at four or five in the morning like he does. He loves that time by himself, talking to God and writing the reply in his journal as God speaks to him. Sounds like self inflicted pain to me, but then I know we are all so different and so uniquely designed.

"Please, can I just have a coffee first and then hear what God's been speaking to you about since the crack of dawn?" You'd love the scene. For decades now he has brought me my morning coffee and because he's been awake for so much longer than me, he can't resist telling me things God has told him as he waited and listened, or some other thing that to him is really important. Not everyone needs coffee first, but when you do you really do, and while I'm having it I begin to tell those brand new brain cells what I want them to know. If I don't do that my mind will start to complicate everything. Neurogenesis, it's a habit I have developed.

Back there in Dunedin I was beginning to have a home not just a house and no matter who dropped in they always had a place to sit. I was no longer afraid to open the door; I liked that so much, I started inviting people to our place. Everything has its own reward: it's the law of the farm – you sow it, you reap it. I don't know how I came by the idea, but it made sense to me that I reward myself for completing my tasks properly. What was I, a dog? Well if you can teach your dog a behaviour, you can teach yourself one.

If I have time to spare my biggest reward will always be to read a book. Discretionary time is of great value to me. It's hard to find but necessary for refreshing and learning. In the years of caring for my grandchildren it was harder to find time for myself, but the joy of being with them was the reward, the only one I ever needed. Those years go so fast and it's an undeniable privilege. If it's yours, just roll with it and love it.

Because I'm a reader I have learned from a large number of authors – I'll include a list for you at the back of this book. I've used anything and everything I could find over the years to improve my skills. Many of these writers have educated me on a plethora of topics, by no means only homemaking. Books have been one of my greatest teachers – I read, I underline, I have a huge library of well read books. The book you don't read won't help you. You may prefer to use your device, I just happen to prefer paper. It's a great thing to model yourself on the behaviour of positive and good people you read about; it rubs off I find.

With fifteen minutes a day you can read twenty books a year, and for me these new insights and knowledge will always be important.

Of course everything has changed yet again, and it's more about what we do on our phones and laptops and when we do it. I tend to leave what isn't urgent on the phone and reply later. It's a wonder I have any Facebook friends at all. When we have time to use at our own discretion it is very valuable, but can be easily abused because for one thing our electronic devices keep demanding attention. For me you could say I want to get the job done and do it properly before I kick back. This is my choice; you need to do what works for you.

I started off talking about seasons. They can be made up of circumstances beyond our control where although we want to do things and be available, for a whole lot of reasons we just can't. I found it's best to go with those circumstances because it's true they don't last forever and if we try to fight them or shorten them we can easily lose what is their gift to us. How we think and what we say in those times can have enormous influence on the outcome. As always, gratitude is paramount.

Seasons turn out to be for a reason. If we are able to remain peaceful enough and refuse to be anxious for change, we learn a whole new way of dealing with them that we would never have learned otherwise. There is a time for everything and our staying power gets more muscle as we see those times through. The lessons gifted to us from the unfamiliar can take us to a whole new level of understanding about ourselves and about the faithfulness of God. I have found writing this book to be a very solitary experience. Because I'm a people person, it's been so hard for me to have to be alone and to find myself having to say 'no' to so many people. It's a season for me, one of giving all I have to give.

After a while my capacity increased and I began to study people like Martha Stewart and much later India Hicks, to learn about how to do larger functions outside the home. Weddings, parties, all kinds of celebrations – I eventually did a great many and still help wherever I can, but because of the 'great many' my back has finally refused to cooperate. I can no longer lift things I wish I could, and that makes it extremely frustrating for me at times.

When you're younger you seldom give thought to how it will be when bits wear out as you get older. It's too late to wish I had been a better steward of my own body. Here's a funny thing. I never got my ears pierced because I hate knives and needles, and now every few weeks or so I find myself at the eye surgeon, breathing slowly as he injects me in the eye. I can't say it's one of my favourite forms of recreation!

I suppose now I'm what you'd call a sage, a Kuia, and I can't emphasise enough to please take care of yourself while you can. Watch what goes into your body: you are what you eat. Exercise as often as you can. I find the habit I developed of fast walking or using the treadmill has sustained me hugely so I can be of more use as I've aged. There are still plenty who need help and I love being available to do things for them. I can still cook two meals at once and give one away, and visit the sick and lonely even when I'm not fit enough at certain times to do the bigger things I love being involved in.

Something that's made it easier for me is a small and regular practice inspired by the first beatitude Jesus taught in what is known as the Sermon on the Mount. There are eight beatitudes or life lessons, all fantastic, but the first one always grabs me. It says in a translation I like, "Blessed are those who acknowledge their need of me". Another version says, "who depend on me", in other words acknowledging that we need to depend totally on God to help us be our best selves.

For me it all amounts to the fact that with God anything is possible, and without depending on his grace and goodness, pretty much everything can sometimes be quite impossible or a whole lot harder. It can be done, but it'll wear you out; that's what I've found. I say each morning, "My Father, it's my intention to depend on you today". There's a wonderfully simple line in The Lord's Prayer that brings me peace and consolation. Quite often I just breathe out the words, "Your will be done my Father". It's the thing of amazing grace – it's not just a tune for bagpipes!

Who knew you brought all your previous life right there into that relationship? Whoever coined the phrase 'for better or for worse', they knew! When you say, 'I do', standing there in that white dress, stargazing into those evergreen eyes, one might say, 'Tell them they're dreaming', or at least, 'It's going to take some work'. By now you're thinking what a dummy! When you think of your goals, and begin with your end in mind, it might be wanting to save lives, climb Everest, start a business, raise funds to feed the widows, orphans and homeless. That's admirable but the same basic principles apply. Take manageable steps, do the next thing until it becomes routine, and you will conquer your personal surroundings as well as Mount Everest.

I have discovered sadly that the self defeating behaviours, those little character flaws, need to be faced, dealt with over time and dumped. You know when they auditioned Fred Astaire they said he had no looks really and could only dance 'a bit'. Well it shows we need to listen to our heart, not the words of a frustrated person who only has power over us if we give it to them. Don't let anyone rob you of your goal.

Remember Anita Roddick, that great role model for women who started what became an international venture, The Body Shop, in her garage. In the same year her husband decided to ride a horse from Buenos Aires, Argentina to New York. Undeterred by his decision, she finally found a friend (a car mechanic saving for a house of his own) who loaned her the money to start making her lotions, cosmetics and soaps because the many banks she approached had turned her down. What a decision that young guy made, how brave and trusting.

Well she eventually became a global phenomenon and her stores ended up all over the world. Her social activism meant she used indigenous people groups and taught them skills and ways of productivity. At the same time she learnt from them their totally natural and organic beauty secrets. They used their plants, berries, flowers, earth, clay, and substances from flora and fauna to paint and beautify themselves and renew their skin. Her garage turned into an international empire. She was one of those who believed in giving back to the community and the world, giving millions of dollars to help both disenfranchised people groups and the environment.

It's one of so many interesting stories of what happens when you allow your courage to expand by small intentional choices. One of her great quotes was, "Be courageous, it's one of the only places left uncrowded". I went to hear her speak not long before she died and I came away thinking how great it was that when she sold her company she gave half of the total proceeds to that young car mechanic who was the only person who believed in her enough to loan her the money to get started! Her book, "Business As Unusual" is very insightful. "Give and it will be given to you". It's the principle. The many who have succeeded against all odds aren't the people who say, 'Someday I'll...' – they just do it.

Eventually my manageable steps became permanent changes: if you have a plan, you can have success. I began to realise my dwelling place made it's own statement. Basically someone lived here who cared, loved the thought of home and was grateful for it. Grateful to be a steward of the immense blessing of having a home, even if it was only a little rented cottage. As I began experimenting with decor and endeavouring to make things look more beautiful, I knew it had all been worth the effort of making promises to myself and keeping them.

This is my usual routine. I've found it works for me and it may be helpful for you. Everything changes with our current circumstances and where we are at the moment, what is happening in our lives, but this is a kind of survival kit I use. Because our general routines will be so different I can only tell you what I've learned from trial and error. When you analyse error it can be such a useful education. Don't forget we are not our mistakes and failures:

- I always start the day with thanksgiving and renewing my mind with positive intentions. I do it as I wake, often before I open my eyes to the day ahead.
- I always eat the same breakfast every day – dark berries for

antioxidants, nuts and grains for protein, coconut yoghurt and raw honey for energy. It's my fuel and I never miss it.

- I always have a list going on.
- I exercise most days, usually on the treadmill, but I've walked many times in thirty degree or forty degree heat in places like Texas and Hawaii. I try to choose a shady place in those circumstances and exercising in the rain builds character as well as strength, even though it doesn't feel like it at the time.
- If I'm going out in the morning I lay out my clothes the night before. Remember I'm not a morning person but you will find this helpful if you go out of the home to work each day.
- I have a makeup routine that takes five to ten minutes depending on where I'm going. You don't want to see me without it; small children would run screaming!
- I keep my makeup and meds in separate containers, my jewellery in little dishes (I found silver ones at the collectable market) and those pieces I don't wear often I keep in a tiny set of drawers again from a market.
- My closet is roughly colour coded for a quick dash and grab; not rigid but easily recognisable.
- I or one of us always stacks the dishwasher and cleans up before bed. I mean always. With meal prep it's such a great help to stick to cleaning up as you go, otherwise it can turn into a massive job afterwards.
- I read the back of a package or bag for everything it contains before I buy it so I know where it came from, if it has preservatives, gluten (for me) and the expiry date.
- In general I keep away from the middle aisles of the supermarket as much packaging and many cans contain numbers to extend their shelf life – numbers indicate preservatives and additives

that can cause all kinds of harm to the body. I try to buy what is fresh and in season.

We plant our herbs and eat them as medicine, they are in everything we cook. I have carried old herb pots with me for decades and the properties these plants contain are so healing and delicious. If you find a herb decoration on your meal in a restaurant, don't put it to the side of your plate – if it's a sprig of basil, for instance, it will calm your whole body.

These are just a few non-negotiables that work well for me. It's always a juggle but worth the effort for sure.

Chapter

10

"We absolutely loved being parents
and caring for Melinda and Rachel."

Melinda and Rachel

Eventually my home became so tidy and efficient I was like a reliable Swiss train. Running the household, even starting to cook decent meals, so by the time Melinda made her entrance into the world, my house was in pretty good order.

For the first time since we were married my mother came for a visit to see her new grandchild. She had never been to our home before and she looked around, taking it all in with huge satisfaction. It was tidy and workable, and all those preserved fruits looked so perfect on the shelves just as they did in my childhood. She announced to me that she was very happy I could keep house properly, and obviously because I was so organised, she thought she would be of more help at my brother's home further down the Island. He had two children and was expecting another. Off she went, gratified I was the perfect housewife, her job was done.

Again I stood on the doorstep like a deer in the headlights, but this time I was holding a baby and I had no idea what to do next. When I bathed her I was scared she would wriggle right out of my hands and I couldn't find a way that would stop her hiccupping so loudly. There I was back in my living room, but this time I silently wept while Melinda just grinned and hiccupped! It seemed I'd have to teach myself all over again.

If only my mother had known, but while she was alive I never told her of my struggles learning how to become industrious like she and her mother were. Like every parent, and she was no different given her complicated life, we all do the very best we can. Her best was to love me in the only ways she knew how. She gave my brother and me so much, including my ballet lessons and making sure I was always turned out neat and tidy. That she saw as her job and for those things and more I will be forever grateful.

She never told me of her struggles either. Always remember to interact because kids know a lot more than we think they do and more especially when things aren't going right. The fact was in those days you never talked about anything personal. It could be said it's how I got pregnant a month after we were married, although parenthood became such pure joy. The learning, the reading, the routine I devised began to come together so it brought such a deep repletion to David and me. We absolutely loved being parents and caring for our two girls. The freedom of having a routine in the house and with the babies meant those years were ones of great rewards and preparation for the next phase of our lives.

If you are interested in the whole matter of babies and routine (it's such a personal matter) we found routine to be the best for us so I want to point you to the book "On becoming Baby Wise" by Gary Ezzo MA and Robert Bucknam MD. This information is very similar to how it worked out for David and me, and many of our friends have also found this book a lifesaver.

As the children got older we found we were faced with two major things if character was to be formed well. We discovered teaching and training are hugely different in how they act out. For instance we teach our toddler that he (no gender slur there) should not have pinched the baby. We ask him what's the word around babies? We tell him 'gentle'. He needs to relearn to accept the boundary you just gave him that enables him to respect you as well as the baby, so he repeats that the word is 'gentle'. Eventually he will understand in his own way that what you're steering him away from is the possibility of becoming a mean spirited person in later life. He will see life from a generous perspective more easily. But of course he's learning and he can't resist so he pinches the baby even harder.

This is where we switch from teaching – which you did before – to training. The boundary was disregarded. What will make him understand that to be mean is not good? That disobedience is not good either? He has to come to terms with the fact that there are and always will be consequences to everything he does, including disobedience. Your training, whatever method you choose (although he doesn't know it yet) will keep him safe and help him develop wisdom, and in this case kindness and gentleness.

Teaching kindness and mercy to children enables them to be caring when they meet a person less fortunate than themselves who maybe looks different or has special needs. I want to encourage you to help your children to understand they can sometimes be cruel, if even unwittingly. Explain to them how little things can help a different child. Just a smile, a 'do you need help?' Talk about trying to include them. Anything to make them feel they are accepted. It will take some explaining to your children. It's putting gold into them as they learn to care for the left out and lonely ones. George Washington said, "How far you go in life depends on your being tender with the young, compassionate with the aged, sympathetic with the striving, and tolerant with both the weak and the strong". What treasures to invest in children.

It's been said that making the decision to have a child is wondrous. It is to decide forever to have your heart go walking around outside your body. It would seem to me that this wondrous experience is not reserved for birth parents because if you make a real heart connection with a child, be it your own biological child or not, is beside the point, you care and you nurture and love relentlessly. Of course our heart does have a strange way of controlling us from our head right down to our bank account!

The very nature of care giving has in itself an enormous power to redefine every part of us. It can affect a marriage, a work situation and many of our relationships both within our families and reaching beyond to our friendships. It's not for the fainthearted. How could that little swaddled bald, loud, creature, so helpless, so dependent on us for its every need, be the same one to clarify with such intensity who we really are, who we thought we were and who we wish and how we wish we could be. And yet we who have stumbled down the care giving track all know that little creature is a piece of cake compared to the bigger creature it so quickly morphs into, it seems almost when we were not looking.

It's interesting what makes the different phases difficult and why. You haven't encountered difficult? Parenthood/care giving is demanding. It's such a learning curve and all we want and yearn for is to do our very best for these children who are on loan to us and who trust us so earnestly. Yes we are decent human beings endeavouring to do our best. Think about it. It's good to think back and appreciate what we have learned from our mentors.

I'm a great grandmother now and if I wish anything, I wish I'd developed the best way to listen, which is to seek first to understand then to be understood. Often all the child, or teenager for that matter, needs is to be heard thoroughly. No interruptions or interpretations. It's very hard, very important. Then there's the need that is in all of us to be hugged, praised and affirmed. Remember to praise your children for their achievements no matter how small, even if you have to stretch it a bit sometimes! You get it! Celebrate them – it's like food and drink to them. They can just about live on your accolades and need them more than their daily bread. You know they are not just children, they go on to be husbands, wives, parents and grandparents. Their preparation is our solemn assignment. Be sure the people who care for your children understand that as well.

Here are some things I think every child in our care can benefit from:

- Teach children there is no free lunch, someone had to work to pay for it and not everyone has food.
- Teach them you're not their personal butler or maid. You are not running a multiple choice restaurant, laundry or bank.
- Encourage them to use their minds to process information, to learn and better themselves, and to read to extend their knowledge (look for Leo Busccalia in the list at the back, his story is amazing).
- Explain they are in charge of their own attitudes and actions.
- Train them to be prepared to contribute in the home. Slavery has been abolished. They can make their own bed and rinse their own plate. It won't actually kill them.
- Teach them whose shoulders they stand on, the good and the not so good that is actually their history. If you have adopted them teach them that in Psalm 139 God says, "Before you were born I knew you". God chose them. They are not a mistake.
- Encourage them to choose their friends carefully and listen to their own conscience. Honouring one's parents is the first of the ten commandments with promise and of course consequences.
- Teach them if they borrowed it they must return it in the same condition. If they dropped it they pick it up, if they got it out

they put it away and finish what they start.

- Explain how they can make a difference and be proactive, in that when they come up against a road block there will mostly be a way around it so don't give up easily.
- Explain how developing character first is more important than any other qualifications they go on to get. Qualities like truthfulness, kindness forgiveness, responsibility, resourcefulness, punctuality, tolerance, diligence, loyalty, wisdom and compassion will take them further than getting the ball over the line or into the hoop. If they become famous, for instance as sports stars who lack character, they could lose their chance to be a role model for another generation.
- Teach them to always be grateful and say thank you – a text is one thing, writing a note or making a call is another.
- Instill in them the joy of generosity, that there's enough to go around, not to be afraid to give and share what they have.
- Teach them the work ethic early. In other words give them chores and make sure they see them through properly.
- Explain when they don't understand things regarding a situation it's best to just be quiet and learn about things like culture, mental illness, physical differences, and have compassion in all those circumstances.
- Do them an enormous favour by showing them how the lack of forgiveness causes pain and suffering to both parties. Without forgiveness they will dig two graves, one to dispense of their perpetrator and one for themselves, the victim. Read them little stories like "Man's Search For Meaning" by Victor Frankl. It will grow courage in them.
- If you have the means, take them to places where they can see children with no food choices, no language that says 'I don't like

broccoli, I don't like this or that,' because those children have no food, maybe just a rubbish dump where they have to scavenge for scraps or beg on the street.

- Explain why citizenship – caring for others and the environment – is important.
- When they are old enough to learn about social justice, explain things like child trafficking, the plight of refugees and orphans and many other unjust circumstances so they understand privilege.
- Encourage them to share the blessings and possessions they have with those who don't have those things. To donate, to give, to visit hospitals, to sing to old folks in a facility – to pay it forward because it all comes back.
- Encourage empathy; even babies will cry when they see another crying. A little heart can break.
- And above all teach them to love and serve God who is the giver of every good and perfect gift, and who is the one who will never leave them or forsake them.

It's good to be over protective, especially with devices like TV and leaving young teenagers alone because that frontal cortex still needs developing for right choices to be made. Little things like rotating kids toys for a month or more so they almost have new ones they forgot about. They don't need the latest everything.

One way to reassure a child it's okay to make mistakes is to apologise when you make one and don't cover up your own inadequacies. You're not perfect so don't try to appear to be. Always say sorry and mean it. Never ever withdraw, love suffers long and is kind. I had a dear friend whose parents were deaf and if they didn't want to sign language to speak to him they'd turn their backs on him. He ended up sexually broken and died so young never knowing who he was, but you see his parents never knew who they were either. There's always a reason.

I need to repeat that in my book withdrawal and lack of reconciliation is not Christian behaviour. It shows decayed fruit and Jesus said, "By their fruit you shall know them". The Apostle Paul said, "To the extent it depends on you, live at peace with one another". Talk things out. There's always a third alternative and reconciliation is the true nature of God. It can take time and effort but it was Jesus who said, "Love one another as I have loved you". If they are taught these things when they are young they will develop the wisdom they need for their older lives. Of course all of these things I have had to learn along the way, but I'm passing them on because I wish I'd known them much earlier in my life.

By the time we were back in Auckland I had people I could consult and I was a sponge; eager to learn everything I could about how to raise a child. We never had what you might call a normal life because we lived a large part of it around the world. The girls made lifelong friends as we travelled but they always seemed to slot back into school very well when we returned home. Their education on the road as we went from country to country teaching and leading worship – sometimes to crowds of forty or fifty thousand people in America – became a normal lifestyle for them and we could not have asked for better teachers. They were having two educations. They did their school lessons each day and filled books with stories and pictures of the places we went.

I could never begin to express the deep gratitude we have for Marion, Barbara, Reona, Carol and Philippa, the selfless young women who cared for our girls. Our girls seldom came to night meetings and I kept them in a routine no matter where we were. The security it produced as they grew meant that although it was a different bed, different food, a different country, the basic structure of how their nannies cared for them was no different from how I would have done it at home. Meal time, bath time, bed time, story time, prayers and lights out were a constant.

As our daughters grew we continued with spells of being at home and then away. Rachel had a very crucial part to play when she joined the staff of the Scripture in Song offices, she was David's right hand there for several years. Melinda joined us on stage as we led worship both overseas and at home. We were recording, compiling music books, and then regularly going away leading worship and teaching at conferences and churches.

Back in New Zealand we were always a full house. The girls had so many friends and our home was continually full of people from all parts of the world. Things just seemed to happen out of the blue, such as when the legendary guitarist Phil Keaggy and his wife Bernadette came to stay for four days and ended up with us for a month. So many people from the gospel music scene came to stay. Our daughters loved the vibe of meeting different people and always helped to take care of them. The endless amusing and amazing stories of our life at that time would fill another book.

Our lives continued at the same pace and we celebrated twenty five years of Scripture in Song in 1993. It was an amazing event full of colour and culture which began the release of indigenous people to both sing and play instruments of their own ethnicity. In most cases this had never before happened in gatherings associated with church meetings. It was a time for the treasures God had put in many people groups to be released in worship to him.

Five years later we ran headlong into a situation with Rachel that changed our lives forever. Almost twenty years since her passing I have to say I'm honestly not sure it's something I will ever get over. I have taught myself to live managing the fact that it's true, while after all this time I still find myself caught in the grief of it when I least expect it. She was such a vibrant and creative person who whole heartedly loved God and loved life.

I breezed into a shop recently that she and I often went to together. Suddenly and totally unexpectedly I was overcome with such a deep feeling of loss and pain that I almost knocked someone over as I turned and rushed out the door, so overwhelmed by the power loss has on a wounded soul. William Shakespeare said, "Rough winds do shake the darling buds of May and summer's lease hath all too short a date". A beautiful bud not even in full bloom shaken so soon from our family tree.

I had been acquainted with loss. The first was my grandmother and the order of that, although totally unwelcome to me, was to be expected. I had lost my paternal grandmother Mary (Marija) before I was born. I was to lose both of my parents as time went on. Each of these phases, while they also shook me, were more in the natural order of how I imagined life to be. Both before and after Rachel had passed there were younger women I dearly loved who died of cancer. I found my heart was both fighting the outcomes while at the same time becoming intimate with loss.

There's a verse in a letter the Apostle Paul wrote that says, "We don't grieve as those who have no hope for we believe Jesus died and was raised to life again". This says to me that death is not the final outcome but rather a process that frees us from these bodies that can be hindrances here on earth while the real us is alive eternally. Although it pains me to remind myself of this story of how I dealt with the knowledge that we could lose Rachel, like no other story it has taught me of God's unfailing love, comfort and grace. I suppose my bereavement with Rachel started almost from the moment I found out she had cancer. I tried to brace myself for what the outcome might be, while at the same time I had no doubt she could be cured or supernaturally healed. None of that was really up to me.

Before I relate to you how things happened and the ways I chose to deal with something so out of my control, I want to give you some understanding from my own experience of how to deal with the way other people (often people close to you) react, the things they say and how they cope. Everyone reacts differently, there are no rules because after all we are dealing with the human condition. People who haven't been through the experience of losing one of their own children can't possibly know the depth and magnitude of the different kind of anguish this grief brings. There is no way of knowing how it feels unless you actually experience it. I advise it's better to say, 'I can't possibly know how you feel', than with every good intention but having never experienced losing your own child, saying things like, 'I understand how you must be feeling'.

People said all sorts of things to us like, 'God wanted Rachel', or 'if you had more faith Rachel would have lived'. Someone started singing a song to me as they left my home one day when Rachel was in her last stages of the disease destroying her rapidly. All of a sudden, to try to cheer me up I suppose, she sang "Always look on the bright side of life". I waved her goodbye and prayed she would never have to go through anything like watching someone you love so dearly be so disfigured and actually about to die. The bright side of that is hard to find.

There were other people who blamed the devil because they felt we had spent our loves teaching people to worship God. I guess what I am saying is opinions are not helpful in these moments of our lives, and neither is it wise to have expectations of people. From my experience it's different from any other kind of bereavement. Some people are there for you while some just can't be. They don't know what to say or do and so they seem to disappear. You just have to go with that. Everyone does what he or she is capable of.

So I'll tell you what I did, how I coped and what I learnt. My greatest take away will be the fact that at all times I was aware God was with me and I never felt alone. I always had the grace to trust that no matter what happened, neither life nor death could ever separate Rachel from the love of God.

The maternal heart is a wondrous thing. It has within it so many different facets that can cope with almost anything, yet I found my heart retreated into complete denial when I got the news of Rachel's illness. Rachel was thirty one and seemingly healthy. She had just given birth to her second child, a beautiful baby girl Amelia. Well with all the reluctance and denial in the world, and yet with every bit of resolve and courage I could scrape up, I began sorting through my role in this unwelcome saga that would play out in a totally uncharted way.

Mothers of course are a whole other people group. Basically they are survivors, they fix things, they know more (give us a break), they interfere more and, after all is said and done, they tend to endure more than sometimes their tender hearts can bear. Yet when they truly engage in the nobility of motherhood, to this complex profession they can bring better than best, greater than they could ever imagine, and history is, as it always was and will be, in the palm of their hand.

Someone said, "Motherhood remains the greatest single preserve of the amateur". Yep, if only we were professionals when we started out. You learn on the job and our children all know they will do a better job until they too become amateurs on the job just like us. Yes it is a God given assignment with little need for reward because it is arguably one of the greatest privileges of life. A lovely little aside I sometimes think about is how much she and I loved all things gold. It wasn't unusual to see her with a spray can of gold paint, transforming some ornament or piece of furniture. The bible says heaven is paved with streets of gold.

Rachel courageously engaged in her battle with nasopharyngeal carcinoma, a ruthless, rampant, indiscriminate killer of all it chooses to attack. My role then as mother, mainstay, grandmother, wife, encourager and channel for Rachel's constant and sometimes desperate needs as she suffered in this contest of life and death, was to be there. To be calm, positive and to do anything and everything Rachel couldn't do. There were other amazing people who did the same. They will always have my deepest admiration and love. One steadfast family friend, Sharyn, tirelessly tended to Rachel's physical needs, bringing humour as well in some very dark moments.

David had a unique bond with Rachel. They were very alike and shared a strong and uncomplicated faith. Together they believed God could do anything. His suffering was quiet and pained. Melinda, while enduring through her own battles with health issues, was always there for Rachel. Her care and compassion endured as things escalated out of our control. She was always so kind and loving and would drop everything to be with her sister.

I decided because I was both the mother and grandmother, it was imperative to try in the daytime to maintain an attitude of strength and positivity to help everyone cope. I can assure you I had to learn quickly to be in a place where I could always access the grace of God, and yes it was my saving grace. There would have been no other way for me to cope. I was so determined to try to remain someone they could all rely on when the going got tough, as it did more and more.

One day I went with her to the hospital when she was to have a plaster mask made of her face so they could do the necessary radiotherapy, along with chemotherapy. As I watched them mould the mask onto her she was so afraid, I longed to be able to take it all for her. But all I could do was sit there and pray and hold onto her hand so tightly, telling her it won't be much longer. I had no clue how much longer they would take to get the job done, I just hid my horror at what I was watching. To watch your child suffer of course is to suffer yourself.

I decided the best thing for me was to get up every night because I wasn't sleeping well anyway. My mind refused to stop thinking of what I should be doing next. Living in the moment was a skill I learned much later in my life, and I'm still learning it. I don't know when I began to do this but I crept down the stairs at night to the living room. For one thing I found it a time when I could regroup. On the other hand I would often just find myself weeping. As I did I began to know, in an almost tangible way, the presence of the third person of the Trinity – the Comforter, the beautiful Holy Spirit. It became a regular appointment between us as we met and there was never an occasion when I felt alone. Not once.

I was surrounded and sheltered. Often I'd just prostrate myself on the floor, I had such gratitude and respect for the awesome greatness of God. I would often say, "I trust you", because that's how I felt. I knew there was a bigger picture although I had no idea what it was, but to trust for me was a choice I will never regret to this day. I still make the same choice to trust God because it is my reality. The Spirit of God dispenses comfort like no other and brings a peace that supersedes all human understanding. I garnered strength to face another day.

I would not be telling you the truth if I said I never postured and pleaded with God over the situation as only a mother would. I felt very fragile and sometimes afraid, and I tried every way to reason with God my father. I reminded him about Rachel's children because who would love them like her? A mother's love is fierce and fervent. I tried the reputation thing, "If she's healed God, there will be glory brought to your name". I went on about all her pursuits. She was going to start a magazine for women and had such influence amongst her peers it would seem a terrible waste of such a vital person. All the while I made my petitions to God, the Holy Spirit just seemed to hold me as I processed the ancient knowledge: the fact that there is a time to be born and a time to die. I had to face any possible outcome and I slowly began to accept the reality that death would never be the end but rather the beginning.

At one of those times while I lay on the floor in the night, I came to the realisation that I was living out an eternal story far beyond my mortal understanding. A different kind of peace seemed to invade my very being, every part of me, to where I knew I could truly trust God with the outcome. I had always said, "I trust you", and suddenly I became in touch with the reality of that statement I'd made over and over. It wasn't just a resignation to the possible outcome, it was what I can only describe as divine knowledge, because when God speaks to us it's on eternal terms. The Triune God is the Alpha and Omega... the beginning and the end.

I felt myself capitulate to that infinite omniscience of wisdom and knowledge so far beyond my own humanity that I jumped to my feet and saluted God, you know, hand to forehead. I said with absolute certainty to God, "You are sovereign". I was getting a glimpse of an eternal perspective. I knew because I was looking at a far bigger picture. Amongst all the anguish, all my anguish, there was hope because Almighty God in his great love will have the final say. The government will be upon his shoulders.

It was as though two things happened to me. I was certain God had the power to carry this burden for me. At the same time I had the gut wrenching knowledge that my beloved amazing Rachel was God's child not mine, and she was going to be with the father she loved so much, forever. I had to let her go and in that moment I finally found my peace. My whole body let my God take the weight of it. My heart was racing but a new and assuring tranquillity swept over my soul. No one has ever measured, not even poets, how much the human heart can hold. I held that knowledge, knew the weight of it, and at the same time knew God was holding me and holding her with strength and tenderness. It was a bittersweet experience.

Rachel felt she should prepare much as Queen Esther in the bible did. She was readying herself to make a petition to her God about her situation. In her final days, with all her courage and faith, she wrote her finest ever speech. As she scribbled her message to God telling of her travail, she could hardly write, speak, swallow or hear, she told him of her trust in him, indented with thanksgiving. It was truly heroic. Her face had become so unrecognisable; the cancer was unforgiving and horrendous. She would submit to the outcome, and I was a witness to the fact that she truly did.

My beloved friend Landa said something so beautiful to her one night. Rachel asked her, "Do you think I'm going to die?" Landa looked at Rachel squarely and said, "Rachel, you win either way! If you stay God is with you, if you go God will be with you". She finally summoned the faith and pure courage to present that petition to God on July 9th of the year 2000. She knew, just as Queen Esther knew, that she would either live or die.

God received her into his divine presence that night. As I sat beside her lifeless body, her soft, beautiful hand still warm as I held it, the mother in me struggling to reconcile anything; I did what I had done all the way through. As rivers coursed down my cheeks, I thanked God for the incredible thirty three years she had lived and influenced so many, particularly so many young women.

My heart was utterly broken but in another incongruous way I was relieved her battle was over, yet I knew then and I know now that nothing could ever be the same. Life can only be understood backwards but it must be lived forwards. I had to make the choice to go forward while at times I was only stumbling in the grace of a day. My precious friend Cindy wrote these words in one of her songs:

"I press on
I pursue
Seize the day
Follow you."
©2007 Cindy Ruakere

It is another choice you make. It didn't come easy for me; the loss has been enormous in so many ways. The gain is a blessing in other ways because the gift of a broken heart is a treasure to be nurtured and used to soothe another broken heart, and I cherish that reasoning. I wrote a song as well that will always be my truth:

"You are the source of all mercy
You comfort my distress
So when I comfort others
I show your tenderness
You were the one to suffer
I was the one to gain
And as I seek to comfort
I find joy even in my pain."
© 2007 New Sound Publishing Ltd.

I love this poignant piece written by the Lebanese American Kahlil Gilbran:

"And when you reach the mountain top then you begin
to climb
And when the earth receives your limbs then you shall
truly dance."

"Lead the people to me."
Chapter 11

SCRIPTURE IN SONG

Scripture In Song

When we moved back to Auckland it wasn't to any fanfare. After all we had been gone for a long time, but for me, even in midwinter, I could smell the flowers.

We had been replaced on the circuit, new singers, same old songs but probably sung a lot better than we had done earlier. We seemed to be pretty much forgotten until out of the blue a bible teacher – a hero of the faith who eventually became a very close friend of ours, Derek Prince, was about to arrive in town. The organisers wanted a musical number before he preached his week of meetings. Radical new stuff about healing, open handed giving and forgiving, how to be free from all kinds of oppression and depression – what caused a lot of it. That kind of thing. New and exciting. There was a feeling in the air that the status quo of church as we knew it was changing.

What we didn't know of course was that the same revelation was beginning to percolate around the world and, as I explained when I began my story, we got caught up in the undertow. Someone who remembered us and knew we were back in town, called David to ask if we would sing at those meetings before Derek brought his message each night. David put down the phone and came into the bedroom of our new home.

His aunt had loaned us a thousand pounds for a deposit on a house. It was an old villa we bought for about seven thousand pounds. It needed a lot of work but we were young and David had a good steady job as the new manager of the Auckland branch of a well known tea company. We had a new company car, two lovely young girls – Melinda was two and Rachel just a few months old. We were fixing things up. David had planted a massive vegetable garden that fed half the neighbourhood. It was a different time, families helping families was just what everyone did. We all looked after the older folks (I'm grateful I still have the energy to do that) and those who were struggling. Food was always a good thing to offer.

As someone said, "In a New York minute everything can change". Our whole life – where we would go, what we would do, who we would in a sense become – all happened right there as David put down the phone, walked into the bedroom and very casually said, as he is known to do, "Guess what?"

He looked at me and I recognised instantly he was about to tell me something I'd forgotten I was waiting to hear. Yet when he said it something in me came wide awake. I knew we had been hidden and sharpened, bent into shape in so many ways. Immediately I realised that what God said to us from Isaiah 49 was what David was going to tell me: "At just the right time I will respond to you… I will make you a light to the nations – to the ends of the earth".

It sounds kind of arrogant and I almost feel embarrassed writing it down all these years later, but in actual fact our songs – which we hadn't even written at that stage – were destined to go to the ends of the earth. I realised how important it was that we listened to what God told us, which was I suppose you could say, "If you shut your mouths and wait, I'll give you something to sing about."

Always know there can be a cost to going against the flow of organised religion; being sharpened and honed to hit the mark can be painful. Would I ever object to what I felt God was saying to me?

Finally there was about to be a fulfillment of his promise to us, and it seemed like the most natural thing in the world. The irrefutable fact is God is faithful. David simply said, "They want us to sing at an event with a man named Derek Prince, I think it's going to be quite a big thing". He didn't need to ask me what I thought, he knew and so did I, it was in fact, "At just the right time". I jumped off the bed and said, "I'll get my parents to come over and watch the girls". I went to the phone and organised it with my mother.

Our dilemma, if you could call it that, was none of the songs we had sung before we had stopped completely seemed in any way suitable. We didn't want to appear like a sideshow; what we wanted to do was worship God using music. We had no reference point. We chose some beautiful old hymns of the kind that gives God glory and honour for who he is then we practiced our amateurish harmonies.

Neither David nor I could read or write music. His guitar playing was of a style his cousin Max Rasmussen had taught him – very Samoan, a peaceful easy feeling I guess you could say. The great thing, although I suppose we didn't realise it at the time (in fact it was perplexing), was all the performance had gone out of us, but crazy as it sounds, God was about to give us something better. The timing was perfect because God's timing always is.

We had nothing to offer other than to stand there and worship with these beautifully crafted words – songs from the "Redemption Hymnal" I think. They had a pianist. We stood there – no guitar, no confidence in our ability after three or more years of not singing in public. It was scary for me, at the same time for David it was the greatest fulfillment of what God had told us. We needn't have worried because it was the beginning of a worldwide spiritual awakening that meant everyone wanted to worship. As we sang we found those who knew the words sang along and, to our delight and amazement, people began to raise their hands and reach out their thanks to God.

It was the beginning of what was known as the Charismatic Movement. In other words no one cared which church you belonged to or for that matter if you'd crawled out from under a rock. People were swept up with love for God and each other. That week, night after night we witnessed miraculous things happening to people. Something was emerging we had never seen before. It unfolded like a flower bud that had felt the sun and knew its time for blossoming was here and now. The beauty, the fragrance of the Spirit of God, was awakening the hearts of people and all they longed to do was worship.

We went home after those meetings and it became obvious to me that David was musing on the fact that there was a huge gaping hole where music belonged. Music that would help to usher in the presence of Wairua Tapu: the magnificent paraclete of all truth, the Holy Spirit. Music to enhance the moment where God the father would, as he promised in Psalm 133, "Command the blessing", for those who choose to live in unity.

What to do? We had heard one song in King James English taken from the last book of the bible. I don't know how we came across it – no google, no nothing – but the thing that resonated with us was anyone raised in the Brethren church as David was, knew the scriptures and every book of the bible it seemed. So obviously it was a natural thing to sing the scriptures.

We tried to find people who could write music. One of David's sisters, the lovely Shirley (her husband Graham wrote, among other books, the incredibly compelling "Christian Set Yourself Free") was a musician and wrote for us. Later we discovered a beautiful man of God, Brent, who contributed to our fast becoming popular repertoire. We took his song, "Be Exalted O God", to every country we visited. It became pivotal wherever true worship was happening. We fished around looking for songs people could easily learn – they needed to be basic with enough rhyme and repetition to make them easy to remember. All good songs – keepers – have those elements plus a good hook you can't help singing to yourself.

Before long I started very hesitantly to try to write some songs myself. You know there's a parable Jesus told about people who were given talents, it's in the gospel of Matthew chapter 25. It's really about what we do with what we've got. If we're talking musical talent and I am, then maybe I had a half or quarter of a talent – sometimes I sang in tune. Because I couldn't write music it was hard to know where to start. I had just enough courage – the sharpening back in Dunedin was working its way out of me – to where I thought I'd try and see what happened.

We were desperate for songs that were no longer subjective songs about 'me and my needs'. "I've got a mansion over the hilltop". Well OK but I'm still here. "From glory to glory he's changing me". Yep we were counting on that but we wanted to sing and praise the one who was changing us. Worship is about what we can give to God not what we can get from him. I asked God to please give me a scripture we could sing. One morning as I sat on the bed I began to read in the book of John's Revelations, the words, "Hallelujah, for the Lord our God, the Almighty reigns, let us rejoice, and be glad and give the glory unto Him".

I falteringly started to sing those words. It seemed to be working so I sang the verse onto a tape recorder we had. Afterwards my courage failed me – you hate when that happens – and I threw the cassette into the trash bin in the bedroom. David found it and asked me what was on the cassette. I told him and he said, "I'd like to try it out with a pianist and see if it works". Well that, I have to say, was the beginning of years of humiliation, as I never knew one chord from another to tell musicians what I could hear and where the melody should go.

As it happened all our musicians for the next few decades were humble, patient people who interpreted many songs for me. We wrote, we collected songs from others, and we recorded. Because the songs were so simple people could remember both the scripture verses and also how to sing them.

It wasn't until 1974 that we met those great masters of Gospel music, Jimmy and Carol Owens, who are now such a precious part of our family, our heroes and our teachers. From them we learned how one really writes a song. You may remember them from their amazing musicals "Come Together", "If my People", "The Witness", and others. They wrote a book called "Words and Music, A Guide to writing, selecting and enjoying Christian songs", on how to write songs for worship. They are, in my opinion, the masters of the art. If this is your passion or your 'call', then that is the book to lead you there. It pains me that they and their family, all of whom we dearly love and admire, live on the other side of the Pacific Ocean. Nearly fifty years of love has flowed between us all.

Pastor Jack Hayford from Church on the Way in Van Nuys California, had stayed with us in New Zealand and invited us to his home where we first met Jimmy and Carol with others including Pat and Shirley Boone. Pastor Jack asked if I would sing one of our songs he liked at his church on a particular night. As I stood up and looked over the crowded building, before me was a community of

Christians from Hollywood. I mean, noooo!! I was thinking if I can just get through this I'll be grateful. I did get through it by God's grace, and I mean that. As I was stepping off the stage, he turned to me and said in his no nonsense but loving way, "We need to hear that again Dale, please sing it one more time". I can't find the words to tell you exactly how I felt but things like 'where's the exit?' would have come to mind.

Our life has been like that. We have taken our songs and recordings around the globe and been on the stage with many of the greats of gospel music who for the most part were worshippers too. Jimmy and Carol's wonderful daughter Jamie wrote so many songs, but one that is extremely relevant at this time is called "The Battle Belongs to the Lord". It's crafted so perfectly. The words and music are so poetically structured, that when you sing it you're in it, you're knee deep into knowing the victory.

Her brother Buddy has written a book called "The Way of the Worshipper". It's one of those books I've read over and over. He has his mama's gift with words and an angel of a wife Lynnda, the Martha Stewart of Mission Viejo Southern California. They are family to us as well, along with Lynnda's brother Bradley, his wife Susan and stunning daughters. I have to say getting off and on a thousand planes is worth it when you have families like this around the world.

One thing David says about some of today's church music is, "The music has become the master, not the servant". To lead worship in public means the worship leader must be a worshipper in private. Therein could lie some of the dilemma. If I had one talent and I used it and God multiplied it, then the odds are you are possibly the one reading this with the five talents. Please don't bury them. God, I found, multiplied what I gave him. The story in the gospel of Matthew chapter 25 referred to above is true. It doesn't just apply to music!

Back in 1968 was when we produced our first record. We did it in four hours on an eight track machine and it sounded like it! All we knew was we wanted to give people these simple songs. We got braver. Because we had used a basic rhythm section for the recording, we decided we would use a rhythm section everywhere we were invited to lead worship. In other words, piano, bass, guitar and drums in church. But what to do? All churches had a pianist on the left and an organist on the right. Oh dear! I'll leave it at that.

To add to our dilemma, our album called "Scripture In Song" – not much imagination there – was not wanted by the Christian bookstores. "You'll never sell those!!" was one of the nicer remarks. We were invited to a Christian Businessmen's meeting in the ballroom of the Hilton hotel. We sang and taught our songs and people flocked to us afterwards asking where they could get them. We had about ten of those little albums with us and they were gone in a flash. The next day we got a call from one of the booksellers who had been uninterested in the album and didn't want to stock it. He asked for ten, then later twenty, then fifty then a hundred, and on and on. We were packing them in our garage night after night.

Our thought wasn't to replace all the marvellous hymns. Our reasoning had to do with using scriptures with a simple melody line so that people could remember them and learn the word of God easily. We have the greatest respect for so many wonderful hymns and indeed the circumstances they were written in by people who really knew God and his faithfulness. I think we were trying to provide a method of memorisation that didn't entail the learning of five verses. To sing the great hymns that have been so important over the centuries is still a wonder to me.

Singing on that first album with us were Warren and Jeffrey Fountain, who with their family gave us the most stellar support. We couldn't have carried on without the Fountains, such people of faith and true mettle. They were forging a path so new in the whole charismatic move, with a meeting each Friday night in their home where so many supernatural things were happening.

At that time David was still working at the tea company and happened to mention to the general manager that we had made the album – always outside work hours of course. David was honourable and devoted to his job, he was also grateful for all they had done to train and equip him for it by sending him to some of the best tea producing countries of the world. For whatever reason, the GM became very nervous that David might get his priorities mixed and end up as a missionary in 'darkest Africa'. He put him through an executive test to see if he was basically worth his salt, where his loyalty lay and where his priorities were. At a classy dinner we went to, the manager had already told me David now had two wives – the tea company and me. I noted he put the tea company first.

Well David took the test and answered the questions honestly, but the same thing kept coming up: 'What would you do in a situation that was possibly beyond your capabilities?' David answered, "I would pray and ask God to show me what to do". It went on and on, 'What if this or that or the other happened?' and every time it seemed prayer or God came into the answer. Basically it ended up with the board thinking David was nuts. He on the other hand was sure it was the only way to solve any serious problem – just pray and ask God. It seemed to him it would be of huge benefit to such a corporation. Well... no! They panicked, realising they had trained a person whose first 'go to' position was God. How pathetic!

The manager started trying to find a way to get rid of him. All he could think of was how to get David out of there. The thing was his management style couldn't be faulted, his tea tasting ability was very adequate as well. He had been trained by the best before the Dunedin company headhunted him. They tried methods to stumble him because they had no legal reason to fire him. In the end the GM wrote saying, in effect, just please go. He came home that night, dropped off by one of the workers. The company car was gone, his job was gone, we had a mortgage to pay and two small children to feed and care for.

That night after David told me, I got a call from Warren who casually said in his standard endearing greeting, "G'day, how's it going?" "Fine", I said, and promptly burst out crying on the phone. I told him David had finally lost his job, which we all knew was a possibility. He came rushing round to our house asking how he could help, what could he do? We had absolutely no idea. Warren went back and spoke to his father, the legendary Wyn Fountain. As a result Wyn employed David in his clothing business, which eventually provided us with the finance needed for our travels, and at the same time he gave us a car.

The faithfulness of God is astounding. The entire Fountain family is greatly loved and honoured by our family and many many others they have blessed. Jeffrey has been in missions for decades and married an amazing Dutch woman, Romkje, who is now a Dame in the Netherlands. Warren's family, including his lovely wife Margaret, have become lifelong friends to us. The nice upside was that Wyn's business took an upturn when David went to work for him.

Wyn eventually wrote a book called "The Other Hundred Hours" about how God can use people in business just as he uses, for instance, an evangelist or pastor. He lived out his message. We went to see him the night before he passed to be with his God. His eyes shone like I have never seen. He was unable to communicate but you knew he could see something we couldn't. Hours afterwards he got his promotion. His steadfast wife Shirley, in my opinion, is a brave trailblazer who went with Wyn where other women would have feared to tread, and got totally involved in all the new and unusual things happening at that time. Now in her ninth decade she is still one of the sharpest, wittiest women you could ever meet, totally adorable.

We were asked to teach these songs at many events and people couldn't get enough of them. They had all the stuff a memorable song needs. Our critics called them 'three chord monstrosities', but people were singing truth and remembering it. That's what was important to us. Northern hemisphere bible teachers were regularly coming to New Zealand from America and the UK, and we were always asked to lead worship at conventions before they spoke.

We kept writing and gathering songs and producing albums. No one was doing anything like that yet, and as I recall there was never a woman on the stage leading worship. I was going it alone down here and in most places in the world where we went. There was always a place for women as far as David and I were concerned, so we decided that's how we would do it. It certainly wasn't always looked on as 'the norm' and it got worse on occasions when I wore pants leading worship with David. In one church, as I walked to the front to join David and begin the service, the minister's son told me that if I was going to wear pants to lead worship he would go home and come back later for his father's sermon. He said, "I can't worship with you dressed like that". There were other occasions, such as once in the US when I was told, "Our women don't dress in pants to lead worship". I had just enough grit to stick to my own principles and I think it forged a way for women in the Church to be themselves. Times change but there's always a price to pay when you're a pioneer and especially a woman.

By 1972 we had just recorded an album called "Prepare Ye the Way". Some of the bible teachers took it to England and the United States, in fact we had agents wanting to sell for us in several parts of the world. That album became double platinum, which seemed a big deal. We went on to get many gold albums and we also got a Dove Award in Nashville. That's the Christian equivalent of a Grammy. It seems strange to some people but we don't even know where we put it and never had the intention of lining our office with the gold ones either. I'm not telling you this out of any kind of pride but rather for us it's where our priorities lay. Some people, and for them rightly so, are honoured to receive such awards.

Our aim was simple. When we began leading people to worship God we had the clear mandate, "Lead the people to me", and to this day nothing else – no awards, no glory or gratification in whom we happen to be – is of interest to either of us. Our deepest desire has and will always be to look out over a gathering of people and see them fulfilling what Jesus himself said, "The Father is seeking those who will worship him". That's all the gratification we need or want and it's why we have always chosen musicians who are worshippers too. Mere performance of any kind has never been of interest to us. God alone is the only one who is worthy of worship.

Someone said "Take praise and criticism the same way, let

it go right over your head and take no notice". There's a funny story with the Dove Award. I stayed with the girls, David went to Nashville. We knew it was a dress up kind of affair and that Glen Campbell was presenting our award. Our big moment was only to be hindered by the fact that everyone in the entire room was in black tie and evening dress – Dolly Parton and all those people – there are a lot of Christians in Nashville. Anyway it was the years of the Bee Gees and we had just been in Australia. The white suit John Travolta wore in "Stayin' Alive" was a happening suit! David had just got one at his daughters' insistence and took it to the Doves. As it turned out he was the only person in the room wearing a white suit, but I found out that the next day one of the Christian celebrities went and got one for her husband.

We had lots of highs and lows with albums. I had songs that sunk without a trace and then others that have been destined to bless people to where I stand in awe. When we produced an album called "Praise the Name of Jesus" 'live' outside, the venue seemed to be a habitat for more birds than people. We wrangled with that album for a long time because we couldn't get rid of the birds. "Everything you have made will praise you O Lord!" Psalm 145.

David finally said, "I'm going for a walk to ask God if we should release it, the quality is so inferior to the studio recordings. I don't know what we should do". He came back saying, "All I seemed to hear was 'If you release it, it will be like a seed and you will see it multiply'". It was finally released and became number one on the gospel charts in England for six weeks. God truly did multiply it. You never know.

All that was going on while at the same time we were doing music and words books, but the most important thing to me in tandem with the music was hospitality and caring for everyone who stepped inside the door. I'd drop everything to make sure someone was fed or had a bed. Our home had been a venue for Youth With A Mission teams since the founders, Loren and Darlene Cunningham, had come for a meal and given us that famous statement of his, "Go means a change of location".

Loren arranged for us to go to the YWAM base in Switzerland. As I recall the base leaders were Tom and Cynthia Bloomer, along with Don and Deyon Stephens who now administer Mercy Ships, a noble and compassionate cause. We were told, "You will be teaching for two weeks". It was one of those situations where we had never done such a thing.

Eventually the French speaking people at Chalet á Gobet in Lausanne were the first to translate our songs and we had wonderful worship times together. Linda Panci was pivotal in the way she toiled over the translations, I'm sure with the help of others. Incredible people, it was one of those 'love at first sight' encounters. It was also where I first met my beloved Landa. Her books about God's perspective on political justice are essential reading. I always say she has anointed brains.

Even better still was the fact that those musicians and singers began to write their own songs in French. It was very gratifying for us. As we travelled Europe the YWAM bases there began translating our songs and then started writing their own songs of worship. Marion Warrington was writing worship songs in German at the base in Hurlach. The leaders there were our dear friends David and Carol Boyd. For many years we were often with them in Kona after David became the dean of the university. Carol, with Barb Nizza, instigated a curriculum for preschoolers for which we wrote forty songs in the early nineties.

What a privilege to be around such marvellous visionaries. I remember being at a mission outreach for the Olympic Games in Montreal. As we led worship we could hear people singing our songs in as many as twelve or more languages simultaneously. It was a taste of heaven.

Back in Auckland we had eventually moved from our original home because I had hauled so much food up so many stairs – it was boxes of food not bags by then. I specifically asked God for a few things to make it easier. Something more suitable (I had a list of course). A pastor came to us and said he had seen what he called a vision. It was a white stucco house with dark blue shutters and a sloping driveway to the door. It had a large verandah (lanai for our Hawaiian ohana) wrapping around the front of the house. I relayed my requests to the real estate man trying to find us a new place, and told him about the house the pastor had described. I asked God if the girls could please walk to school and I could drive the car to the door to offload the groceries that seemed to be feeding half the world.

At least I learned to cook before we left Dunedin. Perseverance, Winston Churchill said, never, never, never, never, never give up. After many monumental failures I had wrestled down how to cook quickly and efficiently – in later years with health in mind. Now if it's not organic, what the heck is in it? Oh, and I want it finished in twenty minutes – true! Back then we ate without question and have lost so many precious people it makes me wonder how much genetically modified food and toxic sprays have to do with it.

Well the perplexed real estate man was then faced with the description of the house we wanted. After door knocking in the street next to the school, 35 Omahu Road became our family home for twenty five years, so the girls were always assured of coming home to the same place each time we toured overseas.

I hated taking them away from their friends, which was the surrounding neighbourhood, but they got a completely different education when we were on the road. Experiences and people they would never have seen or met. Places we went like Poland where people queued for food that always seemed to run out, while officials with guns patrolled the area where the pastor we stayed with lived. East and West Germany with huge barbed wire fences, dogs and watchtowers, such poverty and military control grew gratitude in our girls for what they did have. On one occasion, we were smuggling bibles with the staunch and steadfast Al Akimoff.

Our girls both ended up going to Youth With A Mission discipleship training schools when they were about eighteen and totally loved them. What they learned there became their life standards and a priceless education in getting to know God from so many other perspectives. Melinda went on to another school of biblical counselling and has been on staff at a few discipleship training schools. As parents there is no better gift you can give your teenager than to advise them to do a YWAM DTS (google it).

When we got the house in Omahu Road I looked at my list and the pastor's words, and realised every single box was ticked. It became a gathering place and a home for so many. The pastor parked his car outside the house and said he asked God to show him if it was the place he had seen in his vision. He said it looked identical and then when he opened his pastor's daily devotional for that day it said, from my memory, "Surely this is the place God has provided and my blessing will rest upon it".

It was a huge step of faith for us because we sold the old house for nine thousand pounds and bought the new one for eighteen thousand dollars (the country had adopted metric). We have never really had a savings account, we still frequently find ourselves taking steps of faith. I was nervous and had to ask God for myself if it was the right thing to be so financially committed. I drove our car to the top of a hill in Auckland called Maungawhau – Mt Eden. I sat there and entreated God, "What do we do?" The answer came immediately to me: "I will always provide for you". I went home and told David who already knew it was right.

There was an interesting back story because 35 Omahu Road had just been completely refurbished. As the owner was putting on the last lick of paint, the agent walked up to the door and said, "I have a buyer for your house". The owner said, "My wife would kill me, I have just finished remodelling and she has redecorated the whole house. It's brand new, we even put in central heating and tomorrow we are going to Fiji for a vacation. I can't sell."

The agent kept at it and said, "If I can find you another house your wife likes better today, will you sell?" The man was sceptical but he agreed. The agent went to the very next street and saw a For Sale sign on a beautiful home. He came back, collected the man from Omahu Road and showed him the house. The owner said, "My wife would love this house, I'll ask her to look at it". Within a few hours they had bought the new house, we had bought Omahu Road, the girls walked to school with all their new friends, and I unloaded the groceries at the door. Yes, God is too wonderful for comprehension!

It seemed I never stopped cooking, writing songs, recording and listening to a stream of people – some with the most unimaginable stories, some broken, some lost and lonely and some just wanting to be around our daughters of course. We decided to dedicate the house to God. We got our friends, some of whom were musicians, and had a wonderful evening of praise to God and worshipping him for his goodness to us.

The one night unintentionally turned into a house church, a gathering place for so many to be blessed. It was very much as the first church began in the book of Acts. We all knew where the needs were and blessed each other. It would be our way to do church as it was done back then by the apostles: a home open to the neighbourhood, a place of refuge and comfort, and a place where you could always meet God.

We had communion together, we prayed for each other, people cut their teeth on the gifts recorded in 1 Corinthians chapter 12. The words of wisdom, the word of knowledge, faith, gifts of healing, miracles, prophecy, discerning of spirits, and speaking in a heavenly language or the gift of tongues. We encouraged people to be free to see which gifts they had and to practise and use them.

The group grew so big we moved twice and finally ended up in a church. We lost a kind of reality that had become uniquely us, but people were trained and taught, and as we see them now we are proud of so many. Their foundations are solid and they are like trophies to us because we never held anything back from them of what God taught us.

Sometimes we recorded albums in the States, Nashville, several parts of Texas, including one at Buck and Annie Herrings studio. It was there that Annie, Nellie and Matthew of Second Chapter of Acts, along with Buddy Owens and Jamie Owens Collins wonderfully enhanced the album we titled "First Love". We also recorded in Alabama and California; some 'live' and some in studios.

At one point in 1981 we were asked to come to the YWAM base in Kona, Hawaii. The property there was in jeopardy and the bank was about to take it over. The situation was serious. Our dear friends, Loren and Darlene, trusted us and always encouraged us to lead their people to worship God. Loren's book – he's written several – "Is That Really You God?" tells their story.

Loren in collaboration with David Hamilton wrote another book named "Why not women?" which clears up, among other things, that poorly translated verse in 1 Corinthians chapter 14 verse 34 that says women should remain silent in church. That very verse, along with many other prejudices, has stolen the voice of women for centuries. Women have much to say, much influence and much stamina to get the job done. I've never burnt any of my personal clothing as they did back in the days of 'women's lib', but you don't have to be a full on feminist to prove women have been created with such intuition. Without them things can get very lopsided in so many areas of life where their voices should have been respected. I'd better leave it at that.

In 1981, Peter and Donna Jordan who have always believed in us, sent us an SOS we felt humbled and privileged to answer. Would we come and lead the whole base in faith and praise to ask God if he would make a way for them to save the property? I have to say their daughters and ours became lifelong friends and were in each other's wedding lines. They are another of the families in the world who have truly become our family, heart to heart. Deep love and respect flows between us.

David felt we should record those few days. Somehow we ended up with two of the musicians who had played with Elvis Presley until his death. They had come to faith in God through reading CS Lewis's great book, "Mere Christianity". They told us of Elvis and his kind and generous ways and spoke so warmly of him. Our long time keyboard player – the very talented and immensely loyal Rod Wallace – came from California. Our incredible engineer and soundman was Wally Duguid who had stolen the heart of our girls' first nanny/teacher back in 1975. They are another unique and marvellous family we love dearly, their heart for orphans is immense. They have adopted African children, while their daughter Annie runs an orphanage in Africa. Such stout hearted people.

When sitting outside on the lanai the night before we were to go to YWAM, I opened my bible at Psalm 68. It resonated strongly with me that this was a prayer we should pray with everyone. In fact I felt we should sing it; singing is still the best way to remember words. God said to Moses, "Write a song, teach it to the people and when they turn from me, they won't forget the words". It's a no brainer, something we always did.

I was nervous, I was unwell, something had happened to me – an accident – and I was in pain. I didn't want to let anyone know because there was a lot of anticipation. Sometimes we have to rise strong, pain or no pain, but it was something I'd gladly do again. From around the earth everywhere I hear constant stories of amazing things that have happened as people have sung out, "Summon your power O God, show us your strength as you have done before!" I have heard of groups singing it in the most dire times and it has an uncommonly unifying factor as people engage in spiritual warfare together. This is the song "Call to War":

"Summon your power O God,
Show us your strength as you have done before
The chariots of God are tens of thousands
And thousands of thousands
Arise O God and speak the Word
And all your enemies will scatter,
A sound of war will soon be heard.
A shout your warriors will utter."

I reached in my mind for a way to write this, to do this, and I will always believe only God could have been my inspiration. My great love for the Jordans, the Cunninghams, the Mission; I was so desperate for God to show me what I could do to help them. When we have a longing to serve, God takes care of the rest.

It kind of happened before my eyes as I observed those ancient words come to life for such a time as this. I went inside and told David what I was feeling. He immediately said he heard a drum beat, like an army marching to victory. I knew he was visualising a complete abolishment of the problem through the power that is in the Word of God. That's never been any different for him even though he's been tried to the mettle on more than one occasion.

The next morning people began to gather. All the songs we had planned to use seemed to need to make way because we were truly into what was obviously a spiritual battle to keep hold of the property. Right there we taught "Call to War". On the spot the musicians enhanced it immediately – such pros, nothing to prove, just totally professional and instantly in sync with what was happening. Never underestimate the power of music!

We explained the song to these earnest God fearing people who believed God could do anything. It became a statement of faith and belief in his ability to bring a solution to this crucial situation. Before we sang David read a scripture from the psalm the song came from:

> "Your procession O God has come into view.
> The procession of my God and king into the sanctuary
> In front are the singers, after them the musicians
> With them the tambourine players
> Praise God in the great congregation

Praise him in the assembly of his people..."

It literally made my hair stand on end as I realised we were coming face to face with something way out of our natural ability. We were not fighting flesh and blood but engaging with something unseen as we recognised God's ability to fight on behalf of us all. It proved who held the seat of power. As we led the people, we could never have known the cost of singing our way into the enemy's territory. There was an amazing response; everyone prayed and praised and believed, and God honoured their faith. By the end of the weekend the base was saved and another stunningly beautiful property was also gifted to the Mission.

As I look back I'd have to say that any statement of warfare is a red flag and to go unprepared in the spirit is always going to give a signal to the enemy of our souls. We have learned to take extreme caution and never be cavalier about the forces of darkness. Nothing can ever be said or sung lightly when it comes to battle. This is where it is of vital importance as we minister, to have those around us who know how to intercede on our behalf and who will give themselves to prayer and faith. It's fair to say we had no idea what we were getting ourselves into. It's also more than fair to say that God, omniscient – all knowing – omnipotent – all powerful – omnipresent – always there, has an army of spiritual beings ready to protect us at all times and we need to be very quick to make use of these angelic provisions.

If you are going to lead people into any kind of spiritual warfare to see God use his almighty power to take down the strongholds that surround us, then use all the weapons and the armour of God at your disposal to cover your back. It's not God who brings fear; it is the oldest and most commonly used weapon in our enemy's arsenal. Right from the beginning in the Garden of Eden that sneaky question the enemy of our souls posed, "Has God said?" can put fear front and centre of what happens next.

Our very good friend Judson Cornwall told us of a dream he had on three consecutive nights. In the dream he was in a prison cell and God said to him, "Judson, the door is open, step out you are free". As he stepped out he said he could hear the roaring of a lion at the other end of the walkway. He was so afraid he ran back into his cell and quickly shut the door. For the next two nights he had the same dream but the second night he walked a little distance further and the roar became louder. He rushed back to his cell.

On the third night God said, "Judson this is your final chance, trust me and walk out", so he falteringly walked out while the other prisoners called out to him, "Go Judson, go!" The roaring became louder and louder but he kept going, all the while asking God to save him. As he stepped out into the light he looked to see where the lion was. All he saw was a tape recorder. God said to him, "The only power your spiritual enemy has over you is the power of deception. He used it back in the Garden of Eden and will always use it as his most powerful weapon".

The good news is that most often whenever God appears in the bible, his standard greeting is, "Don't be afraid". That's not just, "Hello how are you", it is what it says it is, "Don't be afraid." If you find yourself afraid or anxious, do what Jesus did when he was tempted out in the wilderness before he began his ministry, as recorded in the gospel of Luke chapter 4. Jesus always responded the same way. After each accusation he said, "It is written".

Scripture is alive, powerful and sharp. In place of "I'm afraid", I find the way to dissipate fear is to do the same thing as our Lord Jesus: "It is written, God has not given me a spirit of fear, but of power and love and a sound/rational mind". Another way to help combat fear that can lead to anxiety and even panic is to get on a roll of gratitude. It's always true that gratitude has the winning hand. Fear and gratitude can't coexist. I know I'm repeating it because it can't be said often enough.

Our Father God has in his divine provision given us everything and every way to make it successfully and victoriously through the privilege of life on earth. I am living proof that from my fractured beginnings to this very day, we have all the equipment we will ever need to enable us to live, love, learn and leave a legacy.

David and Dale starting out.

Receiving a gold album.

Releasing 'A Sound of Joy' album.

David and Dale 1970s when we recorded 'All thy works shall praise Thee'.

Drummer Tony Hopkins.

David and Fletch Wiley arranging.

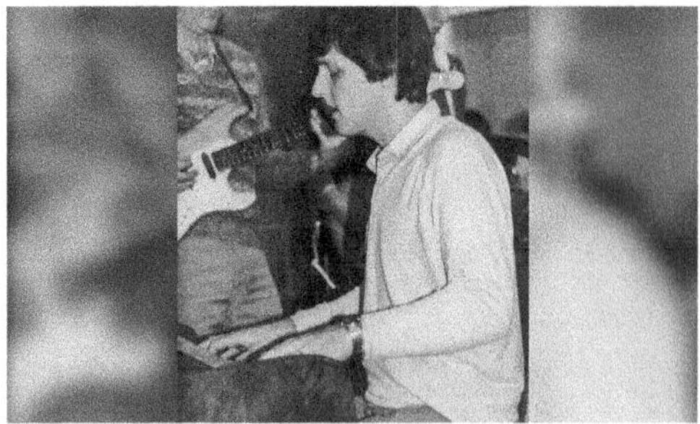

Pianist Bruce Bremner.

Luke Kaa Morgan recording 'Coming Home'.

David with Kings Kids Atlanta, Georgia.

Youth with a mission founder Loren Cunningham with Peter Jordan and the Garratts.

Rod Wallace, Jerry Scheff and Ron Tutt from Elvis Presley's band who recorded 'Call to War' with us at YWAM.

David and Dale leading 'Summon your Power O God'.

YWAM Pavilion where 'Call to War' was recorded.

Judson Cornwall with David.

David and Dale at Holy Trinity Cathedral, Auckland.

David and Dale's ordination as pastors in Honolulu.

Chapter 12

"He heard the word 'culture'"

Commerce to Culture

I want to bring you into our future and show you briefly how we, and especially David, are seeing the way things are changing and becoming more of a reality in the arena of culture. He sees this as being a time for dominated indigenous peoples to take places of authority and honour that colonial and imperial viewpoints have disallowed.

When David was in his twenties he went off somewhere alone to fast and pray and ask God what he should do with his life. David prayed and waited and fasted and prayed and waited. In the end, after a few days, he clearly got the message. It was a scripture from a letter the apostle Paul wrote to Timothy, a young disciple of his. He told him, "The things you have learned from me, teach to faithful and trustworthy people who will in turn teach these truths to others". Although David didn't understand at the time, this scripture was to become a very large part of his life's call and his life's work.

I love what Eckhardt Tolle says; he is a wise man. He believes in different foundational truths than I do, but I never throw the baby out with the bath water. He says instead of asking, 'what do I want from life?', a more powerful question is 'what does life want from me?'.

In 1987 David took with him a group of musicians and songwriters to a beach house. He was doing what God had told him from Paul's instruction to Timothy. On that weekend, as he and those young men walked on the beach, David had an unusual and very different sense of what he felt God was saying to him. He heard the word "culture". It was simple, but has gone on to shape his future in a way that has been so profound he has chased after it ever since.

At the same time he began to understand that if he was to be of value to God in the days ahead, he would need to know the cultural ways of our host people, the Maori. David sought out a humble man, Norman Tawhiao. This man, a kaumatua highly respected among Maori, took him to various marae (meeting houses) and gatherings where David just listened and learned and began to understand the broken heart of indigenous people.

By the way, in so many different situations those he mentored then have done great things from what they learned in those days. We always invited some of them to travel with us, and David made decisive opportunities for them to lead worship, to write songs and to learn from him. He gathered many more along the way as we travelled overseas. Now as I write he is seeking out, as he has done for many years, men and women of other cultures to bring what he calls their 'treasures' to God.

The journey has been both welcomed and shunned. Undaunted, he seeks out those who will sing, dance, play instruments, and celebrate the gifts their Creator has put in them for worship to him, so various controlling white cultures can no longer ignore the marvel of how God made ethnicity.

David has travelled to many lands, sometimes taking a few of our Maori men with him to see first hand how disenfranchised the host peoples of other nations are. The stealing of land, the disrespect for cultural ways God has deposited into these people groups who have had to submit to injustice. He has watched as feathers and beads of Native Americans have been labelled demonic, the didgeridoo of the Australian Aboriginal people devalued and disallowed in the church. So much injustice, the story is too long and involved to tell here. His cousin, John Dawson, is also following a similar path in a very purposeful and loving way, as are several others.

In Hawaii over our decades of being there on and off, we have seen a generation arise who are pursuing and recapturing their heritage, speaking the language and standing tall in their ascendency of the Islands. When I read the hauntingly beautiful book "The last Aloha", my heart broke and ached as I realised how mercilessly such a sacred and beautiful culture was disregarded so heedlessly.

It is the same in New Zealand and the United States mainland, where colonialism has dominated the host people and their ways have been devalued. The colonial powers' main objective was to acquire land by any means. A Native American once said to David, "You and I look at land differently. I want to have access to it, you want to own it".

A great book to read telling of William Penn's life and his humane interaction with native Americans is "The Seed of a Nation" by Darrell Fields. It explains the unusually high level of honour and integrity required to interact with the host culture and keep covenants, to not only uphold their rights within a treaty, but also respect their humanity and identity.

In New Zealand this current generation is beginning to speak Te Reo Maori once again, and the dignity of the culture and all it has to offer is being restored bit by bit. Another insightful book to read is "Tears of Rangi" by Anne Salmond.

David has what I call a brown heart and is forever seeking out people to learn from. He considers a very knowledgeable man,

Bradford Haami, as his mentor. Dr Alistair Reese, an activist who speaks the language fluently, is a close friend who understands the history and current predicament of Aotearoa.

David is of the belief that the shape of the church as we know it will change. Leadership from indigenous peoples is emerging inclusive of every tribe, every voice, every sound that God has exquisitely deposited in all people groups. His DVD, "Let my People Go", is worth watching if this is something you care about.

This is where David's heart is. It's what he actively looks for and encourages. Such beauty and exotic offerings of praise to God hidden for centuries; offerings the church as it exists has rarely experienced.

When we celebrated twenty five years of Scripture in Song back in 1993, David visited every church he could find in Auckland whose first language was not English. He invited them to come with their songs, dances and instruments, and show their uniqueness in giving praise and honour to God. Some people were quite shocked and disappointed in us for allowing this to happen. It was foreign and they had no reference point.

Yet an interesting thing happened. Loren Cunningham, made what I would call a prophetic statement when he said, "This time will be known as before 'Oct 1' (the name of the event) and after 'Oct 1'." He was proven right of course, because from that time on those previously hidden cultural expressions have gradually emerged and become more and more acceptable, where previously they had rarely been part of a Christian gathering.

The Cook Island drum had never before been used to praise God in a worship setting. It was a glorious thing to hear those brave men use their instruments to honour God. People were either mystified or in awe of what happened that weekend. David, pioneer that he is and always will be, was greatly gratified to see and hear those songs and ethnic sounds from other nations showing their love for God without restriction or reservation.

I know he feels there's a long way to go before people of European descent will have true understanding of how to recognise the gifts and authority God has given to cultures different from their own. However he isn't one who gives up easily. Pursue he will, while ever he has breath, to see those who profess to be believers of the bible make room for indigenous leadership to emerge as God intended when he brought the Europeans to New Zealand. I hope David lives long enough and well enough to see more of his dream become a reality.

His other great love, as I've mentioned before, is to do with the land. There are many theories about land I've come to notice over the years. Things like it's 'our land' meaning our birthplace or adopted land as we may have come as immigrants. Then there's the idea of 'our land' meaning we got here first and others came and stole bits of it, fought over it, won it by killing its inhabitants. It's all as old as time, but for me it's very much about if we live on it then we steward and take care of it (Genesis chapter 1).

There are the horror stories of people groups being displaced and forced to other lands and other parts of countries. Justice has been anything but just in too many cases. Then there is the actual land that has its own voice. The animals and birds living on the land and the creatures of the sea have an awareness far beyond our human understanding.

As I write we are hearing sounds unusual to humanity coming from the earth and oceans. I wonder to myself are they endeavouring to tell us something we must learn to listen for and heed. Only time will expose these great mysteries for those who have ears to hear and eyes of the heart open to see.

Dale with Kaumatua Norman Tawhiao.

David and cousin John Dawson with an esteemed elder.

David with Aboriginal mates.

Maori Haka at Oct One.

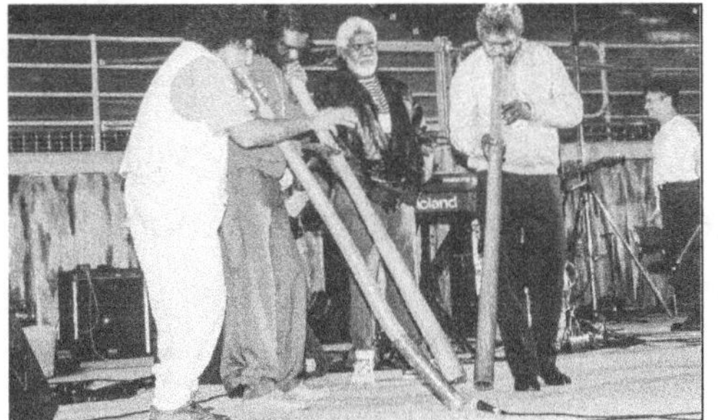

Digeredoo players at Oct One.

The clap sticks.

Vae and Julie Eli.

Some of Island Breeze Kona.

Epilogue

You would think by now, with eighty staring me down in September 2019 I would have bought that shawl and rocking chair, but it appears the time isn't right.

As you read this you will probably be aware that we have just recorded a bunch of those songs from way back. The freshness and beauty of them is amazing. I can't say it hasn't been hard work for us old folk, but the young and vital singers and musicians did us proud. It seems there's talk of more. I feel humbled that God would see fit to use us to do something new – to go back to the future.

You may also know that Melinda and our talented and tireless photographer Brooke are compiling 'Owner's Manuals'. They will give you the scoop on how we have learned about things like food preparation and decoration, some of the recipes we are always asked for, health and well being (learned the hard way!).

Then collecting – how to do it and the fun of it, decorating and making a home, keeping it clean, what to keep for posterity so another generation knows about you. Various things in a magazine format that you can consult when you might need more guidance about how to live a beautiful and abundant life. It's what I hope is handy information and inspiration.

As you read them you will see we do everything on a very low budget, often grabbing pieces of furniture from the side of the road. Our car seems to know when to stop or turn back to pick up a certain handy item we can up cycle. We'll show you how.

I guess you could say David and I never did get the retirement memo, so we look to the future with great expectation of what is to come. With all my heart I encourage you to celebrate your own uniqueness, for no one else will ever do exactly what you can do. Remember you are enough because it's how God made you. I have found if we have the 'why' we can endure the hardest 'how'. Why we love, why we care, why we do what we do.

We keep running into a scripture from our trustworthy prophet Isaiah. He has proven to be very accurate throughout our journey. He talks about the fact that God is doing "a new thing", so it seems like a good idea to get on board and see where that new thing is headed.

Of course I must take those memories with me of how I got here, and I'll keep the hospital open because there are always folks who will need hospitality. Then there's Adeline... to be sure she's checking me out!

In my vulnerability I want to give you the blessing of reading a piece written by Mark Twain. He, although from another century, is recalling as I often do, the beauty and magnificence of the Islands of my heart. After all, it's where my ancestor Kupe came from. And it's where my other precious family lives. Hawaii. No Ka oi.

This is what Mark Twain wrote: "No alien land in all the world has any deep, strong charm for me but that one, no other land could so longingly and beseechingly haunt me sleeping and waking, through half a lifetime, as that one has done. Other things leave me but it abides; other things change but it remains the same. For me its balmy airs are always blowing, its summer seas flashing in the sun; the pulsing of its surf beat is in my ear; I can see its garlanded craigs, its leaping cascades, its plumy palms drowsing by the shore; its remote summits floating like islands above the cloud rack; I can feel the spirit of its woodland solitude; I can hear the splash of its brooks; in my nostrils still lives the fragrance of flowers that perished twenty years ago."

Thanks

I have to say no matter what language I try to use I can't make this word 'thank you' sound anything like how I feel.

There are so many people who have been pivotal in my life and ministry and in some way each of you have been influential in 'walking me home'. Home to where I am now with more wisdom and knowledge, love and compassion and for that... to every single one of you my dear ones, I am forever grateful.

To those who have worked with me on this project I give you my utmost thanks.

To dearest David. Thank you for sacrificing your own time and miles of patience as you typed and read chapters over and over. I'm sure you were wishing I used a computer instead of pen and paper!

To Melinda, what a marathon you have endured for me. It seems like forever, but you never gave up, just kept typing, encouraging and telling me that you loved my writing. Managing your own studies at the same time without complaint, you just kept going. Thank you my darling.

To my photographer Brooke Valle Anderson you went so far beyond your mandate of taking pictures that will make our Owner's Manuals so beautiful. For your serving heart to me, I could never thank you enough. You are a treasure.

To Jan my precious and meticulous editor, you know you could have written the book – your hospitality is outrageously embroidered with the love you and David have for everyone. Thank you Jan that through all the impossible tasks of family life and your studies you made time for me. I'm so grateful to you.

To Jennie and her group of pray-ers you got me through to the end. Thank you Jennie for meals so lovingly prepared for all of our quirky ways of eating, thank you pray-ers and encouragers from everywhere around the globe. My attempt to better another's life has been made smoother through your devotion and love.

To one of my 'sons' of whom I am so immensely proud. Stephen James Hart. The cover you have cleverly and astutely designed has so captured the essence of what I love. Those lilies... you've seen them in my house, and you 'get' me. You are talented beyond your years and have so patiently worked to perfect this piece of art. Thank you dear Stephen.

To Michael and Thelma, who through your never ending generosity have always made someone's life, including our family's, so much more possible with your openhanded giving. You are two selfless and big hearted people. I thank you with all my heart for helping make this publication possible.

To Julie and Leilani her daughter who researched for the Manuals. You and your family were always there for us in Kona. Thank you so much.

I can't imagine doing life without the Kaa-Morgan whanau. You are my cheer leaders and my true family in so many ways. I have the deepest love and respect for all of you. Thankyou for putting courage in me and believing in me.

To Paul Young not only for his foreword which is a beautiful picture of how he has been open to receiving so much of his wisdom from women... but also for the way he has been instrumental in opening the eyes of my heart to the amazing functions of the God

Head. Not only that, but his astonishing transparency as a human being is more readable and accessible than all of his marvellous books. He and his wife Kim and family are such a gift to our family.

To my Redeemer and closest friend, my loving God, is all praise, glory and thanksgiving.

Suggested Reading

In this list I have given both names of authors and in some cases books that have been very useful to me.

Health	Dr Dean Ornish	Reversing Heart Disease
		Eat More Weigh Less
	Dr William Davis	Wheat Belly
	Dr Ross Walker	All titles
	Dr Bernie Seigal	All titles
	Dr Caroline Leaf	All titles
History	Nelson Mandela	Conversations With Myself
	Victor Frankl	Man's Search For Meaning
	John Ehle	Trail of Tears
	Anne Salmond	Tears of Rangi
	Jay Ruka	Huia Come Home
	Bruce Pascoe	Dark Emu
	Gaellen Quinn	The Last Aloha
	Darrell Fields	The Seed of a Nation
Hospitality	Edith Schaeffer	Hidden Art
		What is a Family
Knowledge		
And self help	Donald Joy	Bonding
	Stephen Covey	All titles
	Anne Voskamp	One Thousand Gifts
	Brené Brown	All titles
	Philip Yancey	All titles
	George MacDonald	All titles
	Winkie Pratney	All titles
	Scott Peck	All titles
	Leo Busccalia	All titles
Various	James Jordan	All titles
	Denise Jordan	The Forgotten Feminine

Loren Cunningham	All titles
John Dawson	All titles
Joy Dawson	All titles
Fr Richard Rohr	All titles
Brennan Manning	All titles
Steve Hepden	Rejection
Dutch Sheets	All titles
Glenn Beck	It Is About Islam
Faith Popcorn	Clicking
Jimmy and Carol Owens	Words and Music, and all titles
Buddy Owens	The Way of a Worshiper
Byron Katie	Loving What Is I Need Your Love... Is It True?
Maya Angelou	I Know Why the Caged Bird Sings, and all titles
Wm Paul Young	All titles
Baxter Kruger	All titles
Daniel Walker	God in a Brothel
Daniel Kikawa	Perpetuated in Righteousness
Dr Allan Meyer	From Good Man to Valiant Man
Don Richardson	Eternity in Their Hearts Peace Child
Henri Nouwen	The Return of the Prodigal, and all titles
James Dobson	Turning Hearts Towards Home
C S Lewis	Mere Christianity
Pastor Joseph Prince	The Power of Right Believing, and all titles
A Roger Merill	Life Matters
Roly Houghton	Great is Thy Faithfulness
Christina Noble	Bridge Across My Sorrows
Madam Guyon	Autobiography
Landa Cope	Rediscovering God's Policical Justice, and all titles

MINISTRIES YOU MAY WISH TO LEARN ABOUT FROM THEIR WEBSITES

Kate Rodwell	Dignity Freedom Network... Give Hope for Jogini Girls
Beth Harper	Tear Fund
Pearl Harper	Homes of Hope
Nikki Denholm	Exposure International
Rebecca Walton	Global Tribe
Bob and Kathy Fitts	Alabaster Ministries

BABIES, CHILDREN AND TEENAGERS

Robert Bucknam/ Gary Ezzo	On Becoming Baby Wise. Giving Your Infant the Gift of Nighttime Sleep
Mary Grant	mary@faith4families. org

PLEASE HELP YOUR-SELF

If you enjoyed this book, "PLEASE HELP YOURSELF", please consider leaving a review on the book's page at Amazon (or wherever you purchased the book, if you bought it online). Every review helps other prospective readers to decide whether they should choose to read "PLEASE HELP YOURSELF".

If you would like to be kept informed about future works by Dale Mary Garratt (including Workbooks based on "PLEASE HELP YOURSELF"), please send an email with SUBSCRIBE in the Subject line to more@pleasehelpyourself.co

Please note: we hate spam as much as you do, and will only use this email address to share information on future works by Dale Mary Garratt. We will never share your information with others.